LIVING THE EUCHARIST THROUGH SPORTS

Living the Eucharist through Sports

A Guide for Catholic Athletes, Coaches and Fans

James Penrice

Foreword by Mike Sweeney, President, Catholic Athletes for Christ

ST PAULS

Library of Congress Cataloging-in-Publication Data

Penrice, James, 1961-
  Living the Eucharist through sports : a guide for Catholic athletes, coaches, and fans
/ James Penrice.
    p. cm.
  Includes bibliographical references and index.
  ISBN 978-0-8189-1292-4
    1. Lord's Supper—Catholic Church. 2. Spiritual life—Catholic Church. 3. Catholic
Church—Doctrines. 4. Athletes—Religious life. 5. Sports—Religious aspects—Catholic
Church. I. Title.
    BX2215.3.P46   2009
    248.8'83—dc22
                                        2008038772

Produced and designed in the United States of America by the
Fathers and Brothers of the Society of St. Paul,
2187 Victory Boulevard, Staten Island, New York 10314-6603
as part of their communications apostolate.

ISBN 10: 0-8189-1292-8
ISBN 13: 978-0-8189-1292-4

Printing Information:

Current Printing - first digit   1   2   3   4   5   6   7   8   9   10

Year of Current Printing - first year shown

2009   2010   2011   2012   2013   2014   2015   2016   2017   2018

To my team:
Gina, Zachary, Elizabeth and Nicholas

ACKNOWLEDGMENTS

I would like to express my thanks to Ray McKenna and everyone associated with Catholic Athletes for Christ. This book began with some material I originally wrote in shorter form for their web site (www.catholicathletesforchrist.com), which I expanded here with their blessing. More importantly, I thank them for their ministry of serving the unique needs of Catholic athletes. It is in the spirit of their mission that I wrote this book.

In particular, I thank Mike Sweeney, the President of Catholic Athletes for Christ, for agreeing to write the Foreword for this book.

I would also like to thank Fr. Edmund Lane, SSP, and everyone at St. Paul's/Alba House, for fifteen wonderful years of sharing their publishing apostolate with me. It is because of Fr. Edmund's editing and the work of everyone from graphics to printing to marketing and shipping, that I am able to play a small part in spreading the good news of Christ through print media.

CONTENTS

Foreword
Running the Race (Mike Sweeney)..xi

Chapter One
"This is My Body, Which Will be Given Up for You" 1

Chapter Two
An Athlete's Guide to the Mass 13

Chapter Three
An Athlete's Guide to Eucharistic Adoration..................... 39

Chapter Four
An Athlete's Rosary 47

Chapter Five
No Pain, No Gain 65

Chapter Six
Through the Seasons of the Liturgical Year 71

Chapter Seven
Run to Win—But Should We Pray to Win?..................... 79

Chapter Eight
Body Image 89

Chapter Nine
A Mentor for Catholic Athletes 97

Bibliography of Works Cited..103

Running the Race

"Do you not know that in a race all the runners run, but only one gets the prize? Run in such a way as to get the prize." (1 Corinthians 9:24)

As an athlete, I was always told to do my best and at the end of the game, despite what the scoreboard read, I would be a winner. it was sound advice but it wasn't the truth. Baseball was a passion of mine that drove me to be the best I could be. The problem was that despite how well I did or what the scoreboard read, I was never satisfied with anything I did so I never took time to enjoy the fruit of my labor.

In June of 1991, I began my quest towards the big leagues the day after my high school graduation. I received a few dollars and a one way ticket to Florida to play Rookie ball for the Kansas City Royals. I was disciplined, driven and eager to fulfill my childhood dream of making it to "The Show." I knew the odds of making it to the Major Leagues were just shy of getting struck by lightning; twice! While exerting all I had to give on the baseball diamond, I flew through the minor league system in four and a half years before a call up to Baseball Heaven — The Big Leagues. I had finally done it! I had arrived! I was now playing baseball at the highest level on the planet! My dreams were fulfilled and life was a piece of cake!

Wrong!!! Even though I was making good money, living in a nice home, driving a sweet car and playing baseball on TV every day, my life was a 10 car pile-up on Interstate 5. The dream was a lot better than the reality; or so I thought. Remember the advice I was given as a young boy — "Do your best and at the end of the game, despite what the scoreboard read, I would be a winner." On paper I was a winner, but in my heart I was lost and confused.

Most of my life, I had worked so hard trying to please everyone around me. This list included my parents, friends, family, coaches, teammates and even the fans. Despite how well I did, I never felt like it was good enough. I worked so hard and so long for THEIR approval. This was my problem. After my first four seasons in the big leagues, the future of my baseball career was uncertain. I had heard rumors of being traded to another team, a demotion to the minor leagues and even a whisper that my baseball career was over. How could this happen to me? I had worked so hard and sacrificed so much. What happened to that "winner" garbage? I sure didn't feel like a winner. My heart was in the right spot but my perspective was in the wrong zip code. This is where God used my brokenness to teach me a lesson that changed my life forever.

In February of 1999, on a rainy Kansas evening, I attended Mass at Church of the Nativity. Days before spring training and filled with doubt about my future, there was no better place for me to be on Ash Wednesday than church. As I prayed through the

Mass, I noticed a sticker of a tandem bicycle that had been placed on my Bible a few years before. I always noticed the sticker and liked what it stood for since it brought to life the day I placed my heart and life into the hands of Jesus on my Confirmation retreat. For the first time though, I hungered to embrace the fullness of this two-seater bicycle. It hit me like a ton of bricks that night at church.

As I began to weep, I realized that Jesus was calling me to a place of submission where I had never been before. His whisper to my soul challenged me to get off the front seat of the bike where I had been in so many areas of my life and assume the seat on the back of the bicycle while pedaling my heart out and trusting my savior with the rest. As tears flowed down my cheeks, I prayed to God that I was sick of trying to steer the direction of my life and I was ready to surrender it all to Him, including my career. Rather than playing for my family and teammates, I wanted to play for Jesus even if it meant the demise of my baseball career. As I made this vow to God, the pressure and anxiety that paralyzed me for years on the athletic field was now gone. My role was simply this: to sit on the back seat of that tandem bicycle where the handle bars do not move and simply pedal. Not for my parents, not for my friends, not for my manager. I was to do it for Jesus.

From that day forward, every time I entered the baseball field, I would envision myself on the back seat of the tandem bicycle. Not knowing or caring where I was going, I pictured the robe and flowing mane of Jesus guiding my every step. Whether I was facing Roger Clemens, CC Sabathia or Joe Bag of Peanuts, I was filled with peace knowing that my job that day was simply to pedal for Jesus with all of my heart. Peace filled me in a way that I felt like an Eagle that finally had the ability to lock out its wings and soar. For so many years, I was just flapping my wings.

I'm not trying to preach a prosperity Gospel but this epiphany changed me as a man and as a player. I went from a mediocre big league player (pre-tandem bike) to a five time American League All-Star who set many records throughout the ups and downs of a 14 year Major League career. I also went from a mediocre man to an All Star husband and father of three beautiful children. God is calling you to get off the front seat of your tandem bicycle where you think you have it all together and entrust it all to Jesus. There is a lot of pressure and anxiety on the front seat while freedom and peace awaits those who surrender. Even during tough times on the baseball diamond, I could almost see Jesus above our dugout in Yankee stadium with a smile on His face cheering me on saying, "that's my boy, with whom I am well pleased."

Maybe you have not been to church in a while. Perhaps it has been years since your last confession. Maybe you are in a storm that has brought you to your knees. I was in your shoes and Jesus saved me. He is there for you as well. His Holy Spirit begs of you to open the door of your heart. He is waiting for you in the Eucharist. He is waiting for you in the sacraments. He is waiting for you in the Bible. The choice is yours.

Jesus desires you to run the race in a way to receive the prize. This prize is not a blank check, a trophy that you hang on your mantle or even a seat at Baseball's Hall of Fame at Cooperstown. How can you run the race in a way that you will receive the prize? Here's the answer: Jesus desires that He run the race with you! The prize that awaits those who run the race with Jesus as Captain of their ship is a prize more precious than silver. The prize that Jesus has for you will never fade or tarnish. This prize is an eternal seat in heaven; a seat on the back seat of your tandem bicycle.

"Do you not know that in a race all the runners run, but only one gets the prize? Run in such a way as to get the prize." (1 Corinthians 9:24)

Mike Sweeney, President
Catholic Athletes for Christ
Five-time Major League Baseball All-Star First Baseman

LIVING THE EUCHARIST THROUGH SPORTS

CHAPTER ONE

"This Is My Body, Which Will Be Given Up For You"

These are the most important words ever spoken in the history of the world.

With these words Jesus proclaimed his ultimate mission: to sacrifice his life in order to save us from death. With these words he changed bread and wine into his body and blood—surrendered for the forgiveness of sins—to be food and drink for eternal life. Jesus repeats these words at every Mass, presenting that heavenly food and drink to us.

The Son of God took on a human body for the primary purpose of sacrificing it entirely for us, so that we could be restored to the divine image in which we, in our bodies, were created.

"This is my body, which will be given up for you," is also the motto of everyone who participates in sports. Athletes make this commitment, whether or not they consciously realize it, to their teammates, coaches, and fans: "This is my body, which will be given up for you." An athlete sacrifices his or her body and all that dwells within—mind, spirit and will—for the good of someone and something beyond themselves. As people of the Eucharist,

Catholic athletes make this sacrifice not only in imitation of Christ, but truly in him and through him as branches of his Eucharistic vine. Sports are thus a profound way to live the Eucharist, even if this is one of Catholicism's best-kept secrets.

For Catholics the body of Christ is not simply an image to contemplate—it is our central *reality*, the true source and summit of our life. Jesus' *body* was sacrificed on the cross; that same *body* nourishes and unites us in the Eucharist; we actually become his *body* when we join in communion with him through his Church and live not only in imitation of Jesus, but truly *in and through him* through the Eucharist. Since sports require physical and spiritual sacrifice on behalf of others, they are much more than recreational or extracurricular in nature. When performed in union with the body of Christ, they have the Eucharist at their core.

It should come as no surprise that in a religion centered upon God incarnate—God in a human body—athletics can and should be a vital component of faith formation and mission. Catholicism is a very physical religion, right down to the matter and form of the sacraments; it all began with the athleticism of Jesus.

Think about it. Our salvation could only have been achieved through the passion, death and resurrection of Jesus Christ. Consider the great physical strength that was involved in the paschal mystery. To withstand the scourging at the pillar and the crowning with thorns, to carry the heavy cross through the streets of Jerusalem and up the hill to Calvary, to endure the torture of crucifixion—none of this could have happened without the athleticism of Jesus, whose body, mind, spirit and will were so united and focused that he was able to sacrifice his all.

Like any athlete, Jesus had to train for this grueling event.

Athletics had been generally frowned upon in Jewish culture for centuries. However, in the years immediately preceding Jesus' birth, Herod (of all people, though his motivation was likely more political than spiritual) became the first Jewish ruler to encourage athletic competition, building sports stadiums in a number of cities in the first quarter-century BC. While we don't know if Jesus played any sports while growing up in Nazareth, it is interesting to note that athletics were first accepted in his culture just prior to his birth, possibly paving the way for him to participate.

What we do know is that Jesus was trained as a carpenter, which required a certain amount of strength and physical skill. Before starting his public ministry Jesus spent forty days fasting and praying in the desert, and being tempted to abandon his mission. By subjecting himself to the desert's harsh conditions as he prayed, as well as by fasting, Jesus showed that there is a connection between physical and spiritual fitness. He would not be able to accomplish his mission without strengthening both, and one could not be strengthened without the other.

Athletic prowess was crucial to Jesus' ministry. He walked extensively, and expected his disciples to adhere to challenging physical conditions as they performed their work. In Matthew's Gospel, he instructed them to bring no sandals and no walking stick on their journeys. Jesus climbed mountains, rowed boats, and even overturned tables when he found moneychangers in the temple.

Jesus performed many physical healings, often involving touch, offering his body as a conduit for God's power. We can speculate that somewhat like electricity, healing energy must have needed a strong body through which to pass.

Given the highly physical nature of Jesus and his mission, the Catholic Church has long recognized and articulated the connection between physical strength and spiritual vitality, and that athletics can serve as models of both through their participation in Eucharistic living. We have several examples to draw upon.

In a commentary from the Rite of Baptism in the 1962 Missal (the last revision of the Tridentine Rite before the changes of Vatican II) we read of the athletic origins of the Oil of Catechumens:

> The Christian life is a contest and a struggle against the powers of evil. Therefore, as an athlete of Christ the baptismal candidate is anointed with oil, signifying that he is willing to engage in the contest, and that he is being given suppleness and strength for this purpose. In olden times the entire body of the candidate was anointed, in imitation of wrestlers and athletes who anointed their entire bodies with olive oil prior to entering the arena.

Interestingly, Jesus was anointed with oil just before his passion (Matthew 26:6-13; Mark 14:3-9; John 12:1-8). Though he said this anointing was in anticipation of his burial, it might also have been—according to the custom of the day—a preparation for the physical ordeal he was about to undergo.

St. Paul used athletic images in his writings:

> Don't you know that all the runners in the stadium race, but only one gets the prize? Run to win! Everyone who competes in an athletic competition trains rigorously,

but while *they* do it to win a perishable crown *we're* competing for an imperishable crown. So I don't run as if I don't know where the finish line is; when I box I don't just punch wildly. On the contrary, I discipline myself and bring my body under control, because I don't want to preach to others and then find *myself* disqualified. (1 Corinthians 9:24-27)

An athlete isn't awarded the crown unless he competes in accordance with the rules. (2 Timothy 2:5)

I've fought the good fight, I've finished the race, and I've kept the faith. (2 Timothy 4:7)

In the Letter to the Hebrews we read:

Since we're surrounded by such a cloud of witnesses, let us put aside every burden and sinful entanglement, let us persevere and run the race that lies before us, let us keep our eyes fixed on Jesus, the pioneer and perfecter of our faith. (Hebrews 12:1)

In more recent times the Church has continued to acknowledge the formational value of sports. In 1945 Pope Pius XII wrote in *Sport at the Service of the Spirit*:

Sport, properly directed, develops character, makes a man courageous, a generous loser, a gracious victor; it refines the senses, gives intellectual penetration, and steels the will to endurance. It is not merely a physical development then. Sport, rightly understood, is an occupation of the whole man, and while perfecting the body as an instrument of the mind, it also makes the mind itself a more refined instrument for the search and communication of truth and helps man to achieve that end to which all others must be subservient, the service and praise of his Creator.

In 1982, Pope John Paul II (an accomplished athlete himself) offered these remarks in his address to the International Olympic Committee:

The Church looks at sport with great sympathy, since it considers the human body as the masterpiece of creation. God the Creator gave new life to the body, thus making it the instrument of an immortal soul. Man became a living being; moreover, redemption by Christ turned the human body into a temple of the Holy Spirit, thus making man a member of the Christ destined to be resurrected from his own ashes to live in eternity thereafter. When sport is practiced in a healthy way, it exalts the dignity of the human body without risking idolatry. The Church sees sport as a mighty element of moral and social education.

In 2004 Pope John Paul II established the Vatican Office of Church and Sport, dedicated to spreading the gospel through the world of athletics. In fact, a firm foundation for any reflection on living the Eucharist through sports can be found in the brilliant teaching of Pope John Paul II. He devoted much of his early papacy to explaining the sacramental nature of the human body. He called it *The Theology of the Body*, and in one of his early presentations on the subject he said:

> The body, and it alone, is capable of making visible what is invisible: the spiritual and the divine. It was created to transfer into the visible reality of the world the mystery hidden since time immemorial in God, and thus be a sign of it.

Realizing that the human body is sacramental—created to make visible the invisible mystery of God—any activity that strengthens the body and improves physical health serves as a living sign of God, who reveals himself through the human body.

Catholicism recognizes that our bodies are more than earthly in nature. What we do with our bodies on earth has implications for our eternal life in heaven. God created each of us with a body and a soul, and we will live eternally with a body and a soul. We do not become purely spiritual beings in heaven. At the resurrection God promises to *raise* our bodies and to *glorify* them. So what we do with our bodies during our time on earth will impact the resurrection of our bodies for eternity.

This passage from *The Catechism of the Catholic Church* offers reflection on this point:

> The human body shares in the dignity of "the image of God": it is a human body precisely because it is animated by a spiritual soul, and it is the whole human person that is intended to become, in the body of Christ, a temple of the Spirit. (#364)

The Catechism then quotes the Vatican II document *Gaudium et spes*:

> Man, though made of body and soul, is a unity. Through his very bodily condition he sums up in himself the elements of the material world. Through him they are thus brought to their highest perfection and can raise their voice in praise freely given to the Creator. For this reason man may not despise his bodily life. Rather he is obliged to regard his body as good and to hold it in honor since God has created it and will raise it up on the last day. (*Gaudium et spes* 14:1)

Because our bodies are "animated by a spiritual soul," a healthy spiritual life is vital to athletics, and healthy participation in sports can rejuvenate the spirit.

When engaged in properly, sports can be an actual participation in the saving work of Christ. While this may sound a bit strange at first, the truth is that all good works wrought of sacrifice by Christ's followers carry on his saving work.

Consider these words of St. Paul to the Colossians: "I rejoice in what I'm suffering for you now; in my flesh I'm completing what is lacking in Christ's afflictions on behalf of his body, that is, the church." (Colossians 1:24) What could possibly be lacking in Christ's afflictions for St. Paul or any of us to fill? Nothing, of course, is lacking in the suffering of Christ's passion, for that affliction alone was unique and sufficient for the salvation of the world. But while Christ's act of salvation was completed on the cross, the work of *bringing* that salvation to all people was left incomplete, with the Church entrusted with the responsibility of continuing this work in and through Christ.

So any difficult, good work of ours, any hardship we bear for the sake of a Godly cause, is a participation in the saving work of Christ when we prayerfully unite it to his sufferings as an offering of communion with him, and as a way of witnessing to the gospel. Participation in sports can accomplish this is a powerful way.

Does this mean that it is critically important to God who wins an athletic competition? Probably not. Is it critically important to God that we, his people, learn how to work together as one body, sacrifice ourselves for the good of others, better the health of our bodies which are temples of the Spirit, and build community through whatever means human ingenuity can create? Of course it is. A sport, when engaged in properly with the right ideals and goals, accomplishes all of this. And when it is accomplished through a people faithfully feeding on the Bread of Life and striving to be bread for others, it is accomplished in and through Jesus Christ who is truly one with them in the Eucharist.

If Christ's Eucharistic people can do all of this through sports without consciously realizing it, imagine how much more could be accomplished once this comes to mind! The power of Catholic athletes to use their sports not only as an avocation, but also truly as a vocation, is immeasurable.

Coming to this realization, however, involves overcoming some cultural obstacles. For one, sports have often been considered a less important element of our society, not worthy of a religious connection. Athletes who bring faith to their games are often accused of trivializing religion.

Yet when we truly understand how limitless God's love is

for us, it should be clear that there is no such thing as an activity too "trivial" for God not to be interested and involved. God cares deeply about *every* aspect of our lives, and he wants to be included in our *every* activity. God can be found on an athletic field just as he can be found anywhere else—there is no place we cannot encounter him. Why then can God be sometimes difficult to recognize in activities such as athletics?

Perhaps it is because we tend to downplay sports and recreation as merely a break from the seemingly more important business of life, with no real transcendent value. Yet recreation means "re-creation," when God uses activities outside our usual routine to build us back into the body he created us to be. Former Major League Baseball commissioner Bart Giamatti observed that leisure is, "in Christian terms, a moment of contemplation.... Contemplation is the result not of work but of an activity freely assumed whose goal is to so perfect the self that for a moment we see what lies beyond the self."

Sports certainly fit this definition. Why not use them as an opportunity to explore the depths of our relationship with God?

Another obstacle to realizing the formational value of athletics is that in recent years sports have been maligned due to genuine problems in their culture. Substance abuse, violence, cheating, academic shortcuts, commercialism and emphasis on victory at all costs have tainted the reputation of sports in general. Such a pessimistic outlook is not new. Even St. Augustine in his famous *Confessions* expressed regret at his own involvement in sports: "As a boy I played ball games, and that play slowed down the speed at which I learnt letters.... I was disobedient not because I had chosen higher things, but from love of sport." He added, "In competitive games I loved the pride of winning…. Look with mercy on these follies, Lord, and deliver us who now call upon you."

But as with anything else God gave us to use responsibly, the *abuse* of sport can sometimes appear to be the *norm*, tarnishing its true identity. Athletics at their heart are a tremendous good, from which humanity can derive even greater good when exercised properly and promoted as an avenue of God's grace. A Catholic athlete's mission is to promote this truth.

"This is my body, which will be given up for you" should be the mantra of every Catholic athlete at every level of competition— from professional to recreational league to "weekend warrior." Communion with Christ in the Eucharist and a free, conscious offering of our sacrifices with his, advances Christ's saving mission, strengthening the unity of the body to which we were joined in Baptism, and fortifying our communion in it. As Jesus taught when people scoffed at the widow's mite, every sincere sacrifice— whatever the nature or the amount—is a valuable contribution to the Kingdom of God.

Questions for Individual Reflection or Group Discussion

How do you see your participation in sports strengthening you as a disciple? How do you see it detracting from that mission?

What fruits do you see from uniting your athletic sacrifices to the sufferings of Jesus?

What implications do you see, for your life both in and out of sports, of the sacramentality of the body, and its eternal union with the spirit?

CHAPTER TWO

An Athlete's Guide to the Mass

If we are going to reflect on living the Eucharist through sports, we need to devote significant attention to the Mass, where Jesus gives us this incredible gift. Mass is the most important activity of our earthly life, because it is actually the beginning of our participation in heavenly life. At every Mass heaven touches upon earth, Jesus changes bread and wine into his body and blood, and we are joined to him, to each other, and to the angels and saints with whom we worship for all eternity in the Eucharist.

Nothing else we are called to do as Christ's disciples can be accomplished without the nourishment we receive at Mass. Before we go any further, we need to discuss why the Mass is so crucial, above and beyond the many other ways we can meet and experience God.

It is true that we can encounter God in many ways—a walk in the woods, special time with a friend, an exhilarating competition, and so on. We can pray anywhere, read the Bible anywhere, be touched by God anywhere. In fact, long before Jesus was born in Bethlehem, people experienced God in many different ways.

Why, then, did Jesus come, and why did he formally establish a Church if we can come to God in so many other ways, even by ourselves? Because all these other experiences aren't enough for the *complete* relationship God wants with us, or for the *fullness* of his revelation. Other experiences offer "glimpses" of God, and God reveals himself partly through these glimpses. But until the Son of God came in human flesh, God's revelation and presence among his people were incomplete.

In Jesus God *fulfilled* his revelation, and gave himself *totally* to his people—to the extent of sacrificing his only begotten Son for the forgiveness of our sins. Indeed, our relationship with God could not be complete without that forgiveness, and a way of participating in the sacrifice that reconciled us to God. Pope John Paul II wrote in his encyclical *Ecclesia de eucharistia*: "This sacrifice is so decisive for the salvation of the human race that Jesus offered it and returned to the Father only *after he had left us a means of sharing in it* as if we had been present there."

In Jesus, the invisible God became visible and tangible; God could now be seen with human eyes, heard with human ears, touched by human hands. As such Jesus is the *sacrament* of God the Father, an outward, physical sign of the *reality* he signifies.

Jesus told the disciples, "Whoever has seen me has seen the Father." (John 14:9) Jesus then breathed his very presence into the apostles and sent them out to continue his sacramental presence *in the very same way the Father sent him* (John 20:21), to continue to make visible the invisible mystery of God—in all its fullness—through the Church established upon them and the sacraments he entrusted to it.

So while we can have "glimpses" of God in virtually every human experience, it is only through the sacraments of the Church—and especially the Eucharist—that we experience God in his fullness, and receive the fullness of his revelation and his grace. Pope John Paul II further wrote in *Ecclesia de eucharistia:* "In a variety of ways [the Church] joyfully experiences the constant fulfillment of the promise: 'Lo, I am with you always, to the close of the age' (Mt 28:20), but in the Holy Eucharist, through the changing of bread and wine into the body and blood of the Lord, she rejoices in this presence with unique intensity."

This is why attending Mass every Sunday and Holy Day is an obligation—just as eating the right foods and getting enough exercise and rest is an obligation for good health. If we want to be fully in communion with God through Jesus, we simply have to do it.

But like an athletic competition, Mass is something we need to prepare for if we are to both give to and receive from it. This chapter offers a look at the major elements of the Mass from an athletic perspective, as a "training guide" to help prepare for full participation in the celebration of the liturgy.

Procession

Mass begins with a priest, sometimes also a deacon, and altar servers in procession, all dressed in special garments worn only for this occasion. Just as athletes don't compete in their everyday clothes, but wear uniforms meant only for the event, the celebrant and other ministers dress in a special way for Mass. Their clothing expresses that what is done here is sacred, distinct from any secular activity. The priest's vestments are particularly important. Even if he were to dress in his most formal, cleanly pressed black suit and collar, such attire would not be suitable for a priest to celebrate Mass. If we were to see Fr. John Smith walking down the aisle in his best black clerics, it would give the impression that it is only Fr. John Smith. But when a priest celebrates Mass, he is doing so *in the very person of Jesus Christ*, acting through him by virtue of his ordination. The priest vests to remind us of Christ's true presence and action in the Mass. So just as athletes dress in uniforms to set their activity apart from all others, so do the priest and his attendants.

Sometimes a team enters the field or arena behind a flag or banner symbolizing who they are. Those in the procession at Mass follow the processional cross, a symbol of who we are, the body of Christ. The processional cross held aloft is a bold statement of who we are and why we have gathered for worship. We proclaim that Jesus died for our sins, has risen to restore us to eternal life, will come again in glory, and we are joined to his body through the sacramental life of the Church.

We sing an opening hymn—as well as others throughout the course of Mass—as one body, our many voices united as one. Music—from anthems to hymns to modern day fight songs—has long played an important role in athletics, a unifying and inspirational force to both athletes and spectators alike. Music serves much the same purpose at Mass.

The Sign of the Cross

As Scott Hahn reminds us in his book *The Lamb's Supper: The Mass as Heaven on Earth:* "Baptism is a sacrament, which comes from the Latin word for oath *(sacramentum)*; and by this oath we are bound to the family of God. By making the Sign of the Cross, we begin the Mass with a reminder that we are children of God. We also renew the solemn oath of our baptism." Oaths are sacred statements of our mission and our commitment. For a sports example we can turn to the Olympic Oath and its similarity to what we express with the Sign of the Cross.

The Olympic Oath states: "In the name of all competitors, I promise that we shall take part in these Olympic Games, respecting and abiding by the rules which govern them, in the true nature of sportsmanship, for the glory of sport and the honor of our teams." It seems to paraphrase what we say when we make our gesture of oath, the Sign of the Cross: "In the name of the community to which I am bound—Father, Son and Holy Spirit— I promise that I shall take part in the life of the body of Christ, respecting and abiding by the rules which govern it, in the true nature of fellowship, for the glory of God and the honor of him and his people."

Penitential Rite/Sacrament of Reconciliation

The penitential rite at the beginning of Mass is crucial, and something we need to prepare for ahead of time. Since it is intimately connected to the sacrament of Reconciliation, we will examine both of these in light of their relationship to the Eucharist.

Think about this question: Do you know what your team-mates ate for dinner last night? Maybe not. Does it matter to you? It certainly does, because it affects you. One may have dined on pasta, green salad and a fruit plate, and is ready to compete. Another may have downed corn dogs and chili fries, and is ready for the couch.

You may have no idea what your teammates eat, how much they sleep, or how they exercise. But every one of these "personal" decisions of theirs affects you—because you're a team, and team-mates need to depend on each other. Every time an athlete submits to a temptation that makes him weaker, the whole team becomes weaker. A chain is only as strong as its weakest link. The corn dog connoisseurs are accountable to more than themselves and the coaching staff—they are accountable to the entire team.

This concept is central to the penitential rite of Mass and the sacrament of Reconciliation. When we are baptized we are joined to the greatest team there is, the body of Christ, the Church. We are expected to be a strong member of the team, to train well in order to perform our best. When we give in to the allure of sin we become a weaker member, and thus the entire team becomes weaker. There is really no such thing as a sin that is "just between myself and God." Every one of our sins offends more than God and the people directly involved; they offend the entire body of the Church, the communion to whom we solemnly pledged to be a faithful member. As members of the body of Christ we are thus accountable for our sins to the entire Church community; forgive-ness must take place in the context of that communion.

St. Paul wrote to the Corinthians: "Whoever eats the bread or drinks the cup of the Lord unworthily will have to answer for the body and blood of the Lord. A person should examine himself, and so eat the bread and drink the cup. For anyone who eats and drinks without discerning the body, eats and drinks judgment on himself." (1 Corinthians 11:27-29) Since Jesus paid the ultimate price for our sins with his body and blood, we must sincerely examine our conscience and truly repent before we can worthily receive it. If we do not, we profane that sacrifice. This examination, repentance and cleansing should take place in the presence of the Church community, for our sins affect the entire body, and our salvation comes to us through the body. This can be accomplished in one of two ways.

In the case of venial sin (that which does not break our relationship with God and the Church, but damages it), one avenue for this cleansing is the penitential rite at the beginning of Mass. As members of the body, we can still come together with the other members to receive sacramental communion; however, we must earnestly examine our conscience and be prepared to sincerely express our sorrow to God and the community.

To participate in this rite, we need to prepare for it ahead of time. When we are told by the priest to call to mind our sins, there is not a lot of time if we are doing it from scratch right there in the pew. Sometime before we arrive for Mass we need to examine our conscience and be ready when called upon to offer up in our hearts those things for which we seek forgiveness.

The other avenue for the cleansing of venial sin is, of course, the sacrament of Reconciliation. While the penitential rite (if we have participated fully and sincerely) prepares us to receive the Eucharist, the sacrament of Reconciliation is an even more powerful way to prepare. It gives us the grace of a sacramental encounter with Jesus. Regular participation gives us accountability—to God, the Church, and ourselves. Similar to a medical or dental check-up, the sacrament can identify hidden problems and prescribe solutions. The sacrament forces us to be honest about our shortcomings, and helps us to truly leave our failures and guilt behind.

The sacrament of Reconciliation is the only path back to the Eucharist for a person in the state of mortal sin. Through mortal sin, a person completely breaks communion with God and the Church. As someone who has separated from the body, they must first be ritually restored before they can join the other members to receive Eucharist. A person in mortal sin who has repented and desires to be restored to the communion must be absolved in the sacrament of Reconciliation before they can receive sacramental communion. It is a required celebration, much like the feast called for in Jesus' parable of the Prodigal Son. (Luke 15:32)

Gloria

After the penitential rite we sing or recite the Gloria, the magnificent prayer of the angels in which we join them and the saints of heaven in praising God. Later, in the preface of the Eucharistic Prayer, we will be reminded that when we gather at Mass we "join with all the angels and saints." We do so literally, not figuratively. At every celebration of the Mass heaven truly touches upon earth, and the angels and saints are truly present and worshipping with us. As the body of Christ we worship with the *entire* body of Christ, not just with those physically gathered in our parish church; the body of Christ is that broad and that strong.

Pope John Paul II reflected on this in *Ecclesia de eucharistia*:

> Those who feed on Christ in the Eucharist need not wait until the hereafter to receive eternal life: *they already possess it on earth,* as the first-fruits of a future fullness which will embrace man in his totality. For in the Eucharist we also receive the pledge of our bodily resurrection at the end of the world.... This pledge of the future resurrection comes from the fact that the flesh of the Son of Man, given as food, is his body in its glorious state after the resurrection.

An athletic analogy may help shed light on this amazing truth, that the angels and saints join us at Mass.

We've all witnessed victory celebrations where newly crowned champions hoist the Stanley Cup, Lombardi Trophy, or other professional, college, high school or even Little League awards. In each case the celebration extends beyond the players and coaches who physically participated in the game—wildly cheering fans claim a share of the trophy as well. They did not suit up and play, or make any strategy decisions, but the fans still stake a claim on the prize, and the players accept their claim. Fans who did not wear a uniform shout, "*We* won!"

Though they participate in the game at very different levels, players, coaches and fans are really united in one cause and are all considered one team. Fans play a very real part, but in a different way. Players are on the field competing. Fans are in the stands encouraging and supporting them. But they are one team, present and involved in the competition at different levels.

The body of Christ is more than the people here on earth with us—the body includes *all* God's people, including those who have gone before us to the heavenly banquet. They "cheer us on" from heaven, and their intercession plays a very real part in our lives.

Scripture Readings

Who could ever tire of hearing the great sports stories from history: Bobby Thompson's "Shot Heard 'Round the World," the 1958 "Greatest Game Ever Played," the 1980 "Miracle on Ice," Jesse Owens and the 1936 Olympics in Berlin, Franco Harris and the "Immaculate Reception." The list goes on and on. We love hearing these stories because they are part of our story—those who came before us paved the road for our journey. These stories inspire us, challenge us, teach us, and set a path for us. When we hear these stories it is as if they are happening all over again. Who can listen to recordings of "The Giants win the pennant," or "Do you believe in miracles?" and not be transported back in time to the moment?

Hearing the Scriptures proclaimed is like that. The Scriptures are the experiences, wisdom and prophecies of those who have gone before us in the faith, and are thus *our* experiences as well. The Scriptures bring us back to the moment—or bring the moment to us—which is a central truth of our worship we inherited from our Jewish ancestors. Understanding this truth is key to understanding Jesus' real presence in the Word and Eucharist.

In Jewish ritual (such as the Passover celebration), to "remember" the past does not mean simply to conjure a mental image—it means that an important event from the past is being made truly present in the here and now. When Jewish people celebrate Passover they do not merely remember in their minds a saving event from long ago—they *re-member* the event, as God makes it truly present to them all over again so they can truly participate as well. Jesus gave us the Eucharist in this context, an event which happened once in history but which God makes present again through sacred ritual so that subsequent generations can participate. It is also what happens when we read the Scriptures or have them read to us. Jesus is truly present in Scripture, and speaks to us through it. This is why the Book of the Gospels is often carried aloft in procession, to remind us of Jesus' true presence in the Word.

The Word of God is not a "what"; the Word of God is a "who," Jesus Christ. "The Word became flesh, and dwelt among us." (John 1:14) When we read or hear the Scriptures, Jesus speaks to us in a real and living way.

Homily

The homily is not a sermon, which is why we don't call it one. A sermon is a *talk* on a subject of the speaker's choosing. The homily is an act of *worship*, where a bishop, priest or deacon leads us deeper into our meeting with Christ that is the proclamation of Scripture. Sports fans are not content to simply hear the great stories of the past retold. Passionate devotees want to delve more deeply into them, find the "behind the scenes" stories, place these stories in historical context to better appreciate their value to us today. This is similar to what a homily does for us.

The homily "breaks open" the Word so we can enter into it more deeply and have a more profound encounter with the Word made flesh. It ultimately points us to the altar, where we will partake of the Word made flesh.

The Creed

"Athlete's Creeds" are common in every level of competition, from youth leagues to the professional arena. A written statement of common beliefs uniting all competitors in a single mission helps the efficient and smooth operation of any sport. Once again, we turn to the Olympics for an example.

The Olympics have a formal Creed, which is displayed on the scoreboard of the stadium during the opening ceremonies: "The most important thing in the Olympic Games is not to win but to take part, just as the most important thing in life is not the triumph but the struggle. The essential thing is not to have conquered but to have fought well." The Creed we recite together at Mass has a similar theme. We don't need to "win" or to "conquer" our opponents—sin and death—for Jesus has done so already through his victory on the Cross.

We believe in the Father, Son and Holy Spirit, one, holy, catholic and apostolic Church, the communion of saints, the forgiveness of sins, the resurrection of the body, and life everlasting.

There is a lot we believe, and to believe means more than to consciously assent to the truth—it means we pledge to live by the truth in our actions, especially when it is difficult. The Creed is rich in themes applicable to sports.

We believe in one God made up of three persons—who in his essence lives in community, a team. We believe the Church is one, holy, catholic and apostolic: united as one team, with a common goal of holiness, seeking all people to join us (catholic with a lower case c, meaning "universal"), and following in the footsteps of our founders who were given authority from Jesus, and continuing their mission. We believe that all who have gone before us are still united in Christ with each other and with us as one team. We believe that our failures are forgiven when we truly repent and try to do better. We believe our bodies are holy and will be resurrected in glory when we enter eternal life.

Prayer of the Faithful

No team can function simply as a group of individuals caring for their own needs with no concern for the team as a whole. Teams need to assess the needs of all members and take measures to ensure that all of them are met: who's injured and requires rest; what should be done to nurse an injury; what equipment does the team need; what skills have to be worked on both as a team and as individuals. An assessment of needs and a plan for how to address them is vital.

So it is with the Church. We are not a group of individuals each fending for himself or herself—we are a communion, and we live and die as one body. A careful assessment of the body's needs is crucial, as is a way of taking care of those needs. That's what the Prayer of the Faithful is all about. As a community we identify our needs and pray for them together as one body. The

General Instruction of the Roman Missal prescribes that "as a rule, the series of intentions is to be: for the needs of the Church; for public authorities and the salvation of the whole world; for those burdened by any kind of difficulty; for the local community."

Offertory Procession/Preparation of the Gifts

An ancient pre-game ritual in baseball is the presentation of the lineup cards at home plate. The managers, coaches, or players represent the entire team when presenting the line-ups to the umpire and the opposition. The line-up card represents the players whose names are listed on it and all that they are—the talents they possess and the work they have done to prepare for the game.

At this point in the Mass, members of the assembly present the bread and wine that will become the body and blood of Christ. The people bringing up the gifts represent all of us, as do the gifts themselves. The bread began as wheat, something only God can make; likewise the wine began as God-given grapes. But human beings took those raw elements, these gifts that God provided, and worked with them, using their talents to turn them into something even better.

This is what we do with our lives. We take the gifts God has given us and we work with them, using our talents in union with God to change his raw materials into something better. We then offer them back to God, who will turn them into something greater still to give back to us.

At this point in the Mass we offer ourselves on the altar along with these gifts, knowing that he will transform them into the body of Christ, and us in turn.

Holy, Holy, Holy

We sing or recite this acclamation towards the beginning of the Eucharistic Prayer: "Holy, holy, holy Lord, God of power and might, heaven and earth are full of your glory. Hosanna in the highest. Blessed is he who comes in the name of the Lord. Hosanna in the highest."

The various prefaces to the Eucharistic Prayers remind us of what we discussed earlier when reflecting on the Gloria: that we are truly, literally joining with the angels as we sing, "Holy, holy, holy Lord, God of power and might. Heaven and earth are full of your glory." It is another reminder of the incredible team to which we belong and beside whom we play the game of life.

Eucharistic Prayer

While there are several Eucharistic Prayers that can be selected at each Mass, for our purposes we will focus on Eucharistic Prayer I. This is also known as the "Roman Canon." It is the one that was prayed for many centuries in the Masses celebrated prior to the Second Vatican Council. As such it has a rich heritage in our Catholic tradition, and is also rich in themes easily tied into athletics.

Nine times in the Roman Canon the gifts at the altar are referred to either as a "sacrifice" or an "offering," or both. Our gifts of bread and wine symbolize the sacrifices we all make. Just like the bakers and winemakers who prepared these for us, we have taken the gifts God has given to us, have worked with them to increase them, and now give them back when we gather with the rest of the body of Christ for worship. This is done in athletics when we gather with our team to practice and compete. It is done on a higher plane when we gather for Mass.

The Roman Canon states that we are offering this sacrifice for our team, the Church: our pope and bishops, for all who hold and teach the faith that has come down to us from the apostles. We offer it for ourselves and those who are dear to us, and for the entire family of God.

This prayer makes us mindful of the broader team to which we truly belong:

> In union with the whole Church we honor Mary,
> the ever-virgin mother of Jesus Christ our Lord and God.
> We honor Joseph, her husband,
> The apostles and martyrs Peter and Paul, Andrew, James,
> John, Thomas, James, Philip, Bartholomew,
> Matthew, Simon and Jude;
> We honor Linus, Cletus, Clement, Sixtus,
> Cornelius, Cyprian, Lawrence, Chrysogonus,
> John and Paul, Cosmas and Damian, and all the saints.

Towards the end of the prayer we ask for fellowship with this team, mentioning others by name.

We hear Jesus, speaking through the priest, saying the words he first said to the apostles in earthly time two millennia ago that we reflected on in Chapter One: "This is my body, which will be given up for you.... This is the cup of my blood, the blood of the new and everlasting covenant. It will be shed for you and for all so that sins may be forgiven. Do this in memory of (to 're-member') me."

We turn again to *Ecclesia de eucharistia* for reflection:

At every celebration of the Eucharist, we are spiritually brought back to the paschal Triduum: to the events of the evening of Holy Thursday, to the last Supper and to what followed it....

In this gift Jesus Christ entrusted to his Church the perennial making present of the paschal mystery. With it he brought about a mysterious "oneness in time" between that Triduum and the passage of the centuries....

The thought of this leads us to profound amazement and gratitude.... This amazement should always fill the Church assembled for the celebration of the Eucharist.

We make a request at this point that reminds us of the remarkable event that is really taking place: "Almighty God, we pray that your angel may take this sacrifice to your altar in heaven. Then, as we receive from this altar the sacred body and blood of your Son, let us be filled with every grace and blessing."

Doxology

The Eucharistic Prayer ends with the Doxology, which is Greek for "words of glory." The body and blood of Christ, sacrificed for the forgiveness of sins and about to be shared with us, is held aloft with these words that continue to express our unity and our praise to God: "Through him, with him, and in him, in the unity of the Holy Spirit, all glory and honor are yours, almighty Father, forever and ever." And we respond with the great "Amen."

The Lord's Prayer

A strict translation of the Latin for the introduction to the Lord's Prayer at Mass reads: "Taught by commands that bring salvation and formed by the divine instruction, we have the courage to say...."

Courage is a core virtue for any athlete. Courage does not mean the absence of fear. It means the ability to act despite fears or doubts. Christian discipleship often involves fear and doubt, but we can have courage because of our confidence in Christ our Savior, who taught us to call God our Father. This is how Jesus taught us to pray, with a play-by-play commentary:

Our

Jesus did not teach us to call God "*My* Father," but "*Our* Father." While we each have a personal relationship with God, none of us has him to ourselves—we are all brothers and sisters because we have the same heavenly Father. The word "our" expresses the unity of God's team.

Father

God does more than coach us on the proper way to play the game of life. He does more than officiate, upholding the rules and making sure they are enforced. God does more than train us for the struggle. He does more than cheer us on. God is more than our equipment manager, giving us what we need. God is more than the water boy offering us refreshment. God is more than the booster club providing support.

While we can identify God with each of these roles, he is above all our *Father*—the one who gave us life and who loves us more than we'll ever understand. We are heirs to the Kingdom, his prized creation, and his beloved.

Who art in heaven

God does live on earth, and he sent Jesus as the fullness of his sacramental presence here. But sacraments are earthly realities, giving us the fullest possible experience of God possible on our fallen and sin-tainted earth.

But God lives in his fullness in heaven, and we were made to be with him there forever as the fulfillment of our life.

Thus earth is not our ultimate goal—heaven is. Just as pre-season training camps are not ends in themselves, but a way to prepare for our true goal, so is our time on earth to prepare us for heaven.

Hallowed be thy name

Names are important, because they identify us. Team names are a source of pride and unity. The adage, "It's not the name on the back of the uniform that's important, but the name on the front," says a lot about team identity. Some teams go without players' names on uniforms to highlight the team name and all that it represents.

God's name is holy above all others, since God is holy above all. In holding God's name in reverence we reverence him and grow in holiness.

Thy Kingdom come, thy will be done,
on earth as it is in heaven

We know that since heaven is God's will for us, our journey towards heaven necessarily involves his will, too. Winning a championship involves putting aside our own wants for what the team needs to succeed. Accepting a will that is not our own is a challenge. But as we grow in Christ, our will and God's will slowly but gradually become one as we journey towards becoming one with God in the Eucharist.

Give us this day our daily bread

An athlete knows that God-given talent is crucial to playing a sport—but it is not enough. An athlete has to work to develop that talent, and must be willing to be coached. In this part of the Lord's Prayer we ask God to give us the things that we need every day, but we promise to work with them; we don't expect him do everything for us. God does not give us bread—he gives us wheat to make bread. If we want the wheat to become bread, we have to work with it. God will give us everything we need, but we have to do our part too.

*Forgive us our trespasses, as we forgive those
who trespass against us*

We need to realize what we are really asking God: forgive us in the same way that we forgive others. Sports provide a good training ground for learning how to forgive. There are many instances when we feel that an opponent, official, teammate or coach has wronged us. Forgiveness by definition means we believe a wrong has truly been committed, but we are willing to put aside the wrong and accept that person in love. This is exactly what God offers to us. Do we offer it to others?

Lead us not into temptation, but deliver us from evil

Usually when we sin it is because we were tempted—something looked good at the time, but later we realized it was wrong. There are situations that we know are going to tempt us. We ask God for the strength to avoid these situations in the first place.

Sign of Peace

Thomas Merton wrote in his autobiography *The Seven Storey Mountain*: "Souls are like athletes that need opponents worthy of them if they are to be tried and extended and pushed to the full use of their powers, and rewarded according to their capacity." His point in relation to the sports world is notable: athletes *need* opponents. A hockey game would not be very interesting if only one team showed up; a track meet involving one person would not draw many fans. Athletes need opponents simply to have a competition. But beyond that, athletes need opponents to push them to strive to be their best. While we may oppose each other on the field, we realize that ultimately we're all in this together and we need each other. Some kind of gesture of peace and mutual respect is very important.

This is what the sign of peace at Mass is about. We have our differences with members of our community, our disagreements and even fights. But when we come to seal our unity in communion—the Eucharist—we need to come *truly* in communion, recognizing that we need each other and are truly in this together. Jesus expressed this very plainly when he said, "If you're presenting your offering at the altar and remember there that your brother has something against you, leave your offering there before the altar and first go be reconciled with your brother, and then you can come and make your offering." (Matthew 5:23-24) Pope John Paul II wrote in *Ecclesia de eucharistia* that the celebration of the Eucharist "cannot be the starting point for communion; it presupposes that communion already exists, a communion which it seeks to consolidate and bring to perfection."

This gesture is also a reminder of the peace that Jesus gives, and how very different it is from the fragile sense of earthly peace: "Peace I leave with you, my peace I give to you; not as the world gives do I give to you." (John 14:27) We ask for the peace and unity of God's Kingdom, that it may begin now. This is in a sense a continuation of what we said in the Lord's Prayer: "Thy Kingdom come, thy will be done, on earth as it is in heaven."

Lamb of God

Jesus as the Lamb is an image derived from our roots in Judaism. On the night of Passover, God commanded the Israelites to slaughter year-old unblemished male lambs and sprinkle the blood on their doorposts. When the angel of death passed over Egypt, taking the life of the first-born of the Egyptian families, the blood of the lamb sprinkled on the wood of the doorpost would save the Israelites from death so they could be led from slavery to freedom. The flesh of the lamb became their food to strengthen them on their exodus towards the Promised Land.

Jesus is our sacrificial lamb, whose blood that was shed on the wood of the cross saves us from death so we can be led from slavery to sin to freedom as God's people. The flesh of the Lamb becomes our food for our journey to the promised land of heaven.

At the Passover, God chose physical means for his people to be set apart for salvation. The all-knowing God was surely aware of which households were those of Israelites and which belonged to Egyptians. But he deliberately chose a physical sacrifice through which his embodied people could participate in their salvation. Jesus as our Lamb undergoes a physical sacrifice, involving his total being, so we can physically participate as well. We recognize this sacrifice as we prepare to physically receive Jesus, and ask for his mercy.

Communion

Together as one body we approach the table of the Lord and both physically and spiritually join ourselves to Jesus' sacrifice. Our physical gestures at this point are very meaningful. We walk with hands folded in prayer. We make a slight bow before we receive. We receive carefully and reverently, either in our hands or on our tongues. We return reverently to our pew and kneel.

Dismissal

"Go in peace to love and serve the Lord" concludes the Mass, but its fruits are to come alive when we walk out the door. An athlete trains for a purpose, to go forth and bring the fruits of their training to the competition. So it is with the Eucharist.

An image from a hallowed Catholic sports tradition—Notre Dame football—may be an appropriate way to end our discussion of the Mass. As the Irish leave their locker room and make their way to the field, they pass under a sign that reads, "Play like a champion today." Each player hits the sign on their way out as a gesture of their commitment. We go forth from Mass to play like a champion.

Questions for Individual Reflection or Group Discussion

What are some good ways to prepare for Mass?

Are there certain parts of the Mass that touch you in a special way?

Are you able to see your life both in and out of sports as flowing from your sharing in the Eucharist?

Meditate on this passage from the encyclical *Ecclesia de eucharistia* by Pope John Paul II:

> No Christian community can be built up unless it has its basis and center in the celebration of the most Holy Eucharist. They have a responsibility, therefore, to keep alive in the community a genuine 'hunger' for the Eucharist, so that no opportunity for the celebration of Mass will ever be missed.

CHAPTER THREE

An Athlete's Guide to Eucharistic Adoration

Now that we've reflected on the Mass, this chapter will focus on a popular devotion that is meant to draw us deeper into our life in the Eucharist: Adoration of the Blessed Sacrament. This is the practice of visiting a church or chapel where the Eucharist is exposed (displayed) in a monstrance—a beautifully decorated gold container so the faithful can spend time in prayer and adoration before the true presence of Jesus in the Blessed Sacrament (the term used for the Eucharist when it is being reserved).

This is also known as Eucharistic adoration. Spending an hour or so in the presence of the exposed Eucharist is sometimes called a "Holy Hour." If exposition of the Blessed Sacrament is not available, time before the Eucharist reserved in a tabernacle is valuable as well.

Eucharistic adoration is not equivalent to receiving the sacrament, nor is it to be considered a "substitute" for receiving communion. But those who make it a part of their prayer life find that an hour before the Blessed Sacrament is a great way to strengthen their living of the Eucharist.

To gain a better appreciation of what Eucharistic adoration is all about, try the following mental exercise.

Imagine that you and a group—perhaps your teammates—are gathered in a room, and each of you is given a blank slip of paper and a pencil. On that paper you are asked to write your favorite thing to eat. All diets and training restrictions are off—you may name whatever you'd like. (For the purposes of this exercise, call something specific to mind.) The papers are then collected, and the foods that everyone named are ordered from a caterer.

A tray is placed in front of each person, and the food they selected is set before them. (Picture the food you selected on a tray before you.) Then an announcement is made about the one rule governing this exercise: nobody can eat. You will spend one hour in silence, looking at your favorite food, but you are not allowed to touch it. You will notice how it looks, how it smells, think about how it would taste if you could eat it. You are told to be aware of any reactions being raised in you as a result of this exercise. At the end of the hour the uneaten food is collected and donated to a soup kitchen.

What would that hour be like for you? Perhaps it would be excruciating. You may be filled with such a hunger for that food that it would drive you crazy not to be able to eat it; you may long for your next opportunity to get some, and may even stop at the store on the way home to satisfy your craving.

Or maybe you would not be hungry at all. Perhaps you ate before arriving for this exercise, so the space inside you that otherwise would have craved that favorite food is filled with something else. If so, maybe you wish now that you hadn't satisfied your hunger with other things because you are now missing what would really satisfy you. Or perhaps you would be satisfied with your full stomach, and lose interest in that favorite food altogether. There could be a wide range of reactions in between.

Now let's say instead of that scenario, the group goes inside a church and assembles in the pews. The Blessed Sacrament, the body of Christ in the Eucharist, is placed in a monstrance on the altar. You are told that for one hour you will be in the presence of Jesus in the Eucharist, but you cannot receive him. You will look at the Eucharist, think about it, pray before it, meditate and contemplate it. You are instructed to be aware of any reactions being raised inside you. At the end of the hour the Blessed Sacrament will be returned unconsumed to the tabernacle.

What would that hour be like for you? Would you be filled with such a hunger for Jesus in the Eucharist that you could not wait for your next chance to go to Mass and receive? Or would the space inside you that naturally hungers for Jesus be filled with something else you look to instead of him to fill your emptiness? If you filled that spot with something else, how does that affect the way you look at the Eucharist? Do you regret having turned to something different for fulfillment, and feel your hunger for Jesus returning? Or are you satisfied with what fills you, and would rather be doing something else with that hour?

How would an hour before your favorite earthly food compare with an hour spent before the Eucharist?

At the heart of all these questions is a gauge of our relationship with Jesus and our life as members of his body. Eucharistic adoration is a great place to raise the questions and to search for answers.

Central to all of these questions is the lifelong conflict between our hunger for earthly things and our hunger for the truth that leads us to heaven. Athletes experience an analogy of this struggle. Cravings for foods that taste good but are unhealthy must be set aside to pursue a diet that may be less sensually gratifying but better for the body. In our life with God we need to discern between our desires that seek to satisfy selfish wants, and those that turn our attention outwards to seek him, our real need. This struggle dates back to the ancient Israelites, as does the ultimate purpose of the struggle:

> Moses said to the people, "Remember how for forty years now the Lord, your God, has directed all your journeying in the desert, so as to test you by afflic- tion and find out whether or not it was your intention to keep his commandments. He therefore let you be afflicted with hunger, and then fed you with manna, a food unknown to you and your fathers, in order to show you that not by bread alone does man live, but by every word that comes forth from the mouth of the Lord." (Deuteronomy 8:2-3)

The Word "that comes forth from the mouth of the Lord" is Jesus Christ, the Word made flesh who dwelt among us. We live not by earthly bread alone—which satisfies us for a while but eventually leaves us hungry again—but by Jesus Christ, the Bread of Life who satisfies our true hunger eternally. The afflictions we face test the object of our hunger—whether we long for things of this earth or for Jesus. An athlete may hunger for a banana split, but longs more for victory and what is necessary to attain it. A Christian hungers for many earthly things, but longs more for heaven.

What is necessary to attain heaven is what truly keeps us alive: every word that comes forth from the mouth of the Lord. The Word was made flesh in Jesus, and is given to us through the Scriptures and the Church he established, and primarily through our sharing of his flesh in the Eucharist.

Adoration of the Blessed Sacrament is meant to increase our desire to consume Jesus in the Eucharist and to have him consume us. Adoration gives us the opportunity to assess what is really important to us. Are we satisfying our hunger for God by feasting on other things? Our earthly food satisfies the desires of the flesh; what are our spiritual desires, and what is the food we seek to satisfy them?

Eucharistic adoration requires quiet time, so we can catch our breath in the presence of Jesus and allow him to breathe his life into us. This might be a difficult change of pace for athletes who are used to *doing* something to train and to compete. Eucharistic adoration calls for doing *nothing*—being still in God's presence so he can touch us in places where our usual bustling activity may not allow him to penetrate.

Every athlete needs to have rest as a part of his or her routine. The body and mind will malfunction if they are always active. Eucharistic adoration gives us a chance to rest with Jesus, to allow him to recharge our physical and spiritual energy so we can return refreshed and invigorated to live the Eucharist.

There are a number of ways to pray during a holy hour before the Blessed Sacrament: quiet meditation, a rosary, various recited prayers, contemplation of a Scripture passage, or other sacred reading. The following prayer, Anima Christi (Soul of Christ) provides a good grounding for our disposition before the Blessed Sacrament. It is also a good prayer to say before a practice or a competition, to stay focused on the Eucharistic aspects of sports. We conclude this chapter with this prayer:

Soul of Christ, sanctify me.
Body of Christ, save me.
Blood of Christ, inebriate me.
Water from the side of Christ, wash me.
Passion of Christ, strengthen me.
O good Jesus, hear me.
Within your wounds conceal me.
Do not permit me to be parted from you.
From the evil foe protect me.
At the hour of my death call me.
And bid me come to you,
to praise you with all your saints
for ever and ever.
Amen.

Questions for Individual Reflection or Group Discussion

Review these questions presented earlier in the chapter:

What would a holy hour be like for you? Would you be filled with such a hunger for Jesus in the Eucharist that you could not wait for your next chance to go to Mass and receive? Or would the space inside you that naturally hungers for Jesus be filled with something else you look to instead of him to fill your emptiness?

If you filled that spot with something else, how does that affect the way you look at the Eucharist? Do you regret having turned to something different for fulfillment, and feel your hunger for Jesus returning? Or are you satisfied with what fills you, and would rather be doing something else with that hour?

How would your reaction to an hour before your favorite earthly food compare to your reaction to an hour spent before the Eucharist?

CHAPTER FOUR

An Athlete's Rosary

Another Catholic tradition that draws us deeper into the mystery of the Eucharist is the Rosary. We have emphasized the importance of community—we come to Christ together with all the members of his body. While there is a place for personal prayer, praying with other members of the body, or asking them to pray for us, is an essential component of our life in Christ. We do it with others on earth, but we also do it with those in heaven.

As Catholics we realize that the body of Christ extends beyond the bonds of space and time, that those who have gone before us to heaven remain members of the communion to which we are joined. As such they are powerful prayer partners. None is as special as the Blessed Virgin Mary, Jesus' own mother, whom he gave to the Church to be our mother. As one who was assumed body and soul into heaven, Mary is also the archetype of humanity, created to be holy in body and soul for all eternity. The Rosary is a prayer with Mary, in which we contemplate with her the mystery of her Son and our Savior, Jesus Christ.

Before we delve into the twenty mysteries of the Rosary

and meditate on each from an athletic perspective, let us take a moment to consider Mary's place in validating the sanctity of the body.

When it was time for God to send his Son into the world, he relied on the cooperation of a human being, as he does when he creates all human life. Nobody appears out of nowhere in a puff of smoke; God designed the human body to cooperate with him in his plan to bring new life into the world. The sanctity of the body and the importance of what we do with it is perhaps nowhere more poignantly expressed than it is in that reality.

God sent his Son into the world for the primary purpose of sacrificing his body and blood for the forgiveness of sins. That body and blood needed another's body and blood in which to be conceived, nourished and brought forth. Mary is the one who agreed to be that sacred vessel. Jesus fed on Mary's body and blood in her womb so that he could have a body and blood that he could ultimately sacrifice on behalf of all mankind. Her connection with the Eucharist is profound.

We are also reminded that each time we participate in the Eucharist, everything that happened at Calvary is made present to us. That would include Jesus' giving his mother to John at the foot of the cross. Since John was one of the apostles upon whom Jesus established the Church, he gave her to the Church to be our mother as well. (John 19:26-27) So each time we receive Communion, Jesus also presents Mary to us as our mother. As John took her into his home, we take her into ours.

Praying with Mary as athletes of Christ, let's meditate on the mysteries of the Rosary from an athletic point of view.

Joyful Mysteries

The Annunciation

The angel Gabriel delivers God's message to Mary, and it seems to make little sense to her. "She was perplexed by these words.... 'How will this come about?'" (Luke 1:29, 34) Mary then listens to Gabriel's explanation of God's will for her and humbly submits, though she does not yet understand everything. "Behold, the handmaid of the Lord; let it be done to me according to your word." (Luke 1:38)

Athletes must submit to the authority of coaches and officials, though we may not always understand their decisions. For Catholic athletes this serves as a reminder that we are called to submit to the authority of Christ entrusted to his Church. Even if the game plan seems troubling and confusing, and we might prefer a different strategy, God truly knows what is best for us, for he knows us better than we know ourselves. God sees the whole picture of how each member of his team fits into the entire plan. May our response as athletes and as disciples echo Mary's answer: "Let it be done to me according to your word."

The Visitation

After receiving news from Gabriel about her own vocation, Mary immediately focuses on another part of the message: her cousin Elizabeth is also with child, though she is much older and thought to be barren. "For nothing will be impossible for God." (Luke 1:37) Mary sets out in haste to the hill country (a rather challenging physical feat in those days) to visit Elizabeth. Mary's thoughts are with Elizabeth at this time, not focused entirely on herself.

As such Mary is the perfect model of a teammate, concerned about the good of another even in her own moment in the spotlight. Likewise Elizabeth is focused on Mary and the baby she is carrying. May the teamwork we experience in sports lead us, like Mary and Elizabeth, deeper into the mystery of the body of Christ to which we all belong.

The Birth of Jesus

And the Word became flesh
And dwelt among us,
And we saw his glory,
Glory as of the only begotten of the Father,
Full of grace and truth.
(John 1:14)

The eternal Word of God takes on human flesh at Bethlehem. The Son of God takes on a human body, sanctifying the body and making it a temple of the Spirit. Everything we do with our bodies needs to reflect that reality. "Don't you know that your bodies are Temples of the Holy Spirit within you, who comes to you from God, and that you don't belong to yourselves? You were bought for a price, so glorify God in your bodies!" (1 Corinthians 6:19-20)

The Presentation in the Temple

Simeon proclaims the glory which this child will bring: "My eyes have seen your salvation, prepared in the presence of all the peoples, a light of revelation to the Gentiles, and glory to your people Israel." (Luke 2:30-32) Yet he also warns Mary that difficulties will arise for her as a result of her Son's mission: "He's the child destined to bring about the fall and rise of many in Israel, and to be a sign that will be opposed (and a sword will pierce your own soul) so that the thoughts of many hearts may be revealed." (Luke 2:34-35)

For athletes, all glory comes with a price. Success in competition requires discipline, sacrifice, pain, difficulties and challenges—these are swords that pierce. Mary never backed down from the difficulties involved in being the mother of the Savior. She remained faithful to the end, even walking the road to Calvary and witnessing her Son's death. May we approach our mission as athletes and disciples with the same steadfast commitment.

The Finding of Jesus in the Temple

When Mary and Joseph realize that Jesus is not with them in the caravan coming home from Passover, they frantically search Jerusalem for three days. When they discover him in the temple speaking with the teachers Jesus asks them, "Why were you looking for me? Didn't you know that I have to concern myself with my Father's affairs?" (Luke 2:49) After three days of searching in the wrong places, Mary and Joseph find Jesus exactly where he belonged—perhaps where they should have looked in the first place.

How do we respond in anxious moments when it may appear that Jesus is not with us? Are we expecting to find him only in certain places? Or do we look to other things—athletics in particular—as a replacement for Christ? Sports can pose this temptation. The Vatican recognized this danger in the preface to *The World of Sport Today: A Field of Christian Mission*: "For many of our contemporaries sport has become a way of life, an essential element for meeting basic needs, such as self-esteem and self-fulfillment, and a factor that not only determines a sense of identity and belonging, but also the meaning of life itself. And that is not all: sport has become, in every respect, a surrogate for religious experience." Our participation in sports needs to lead us closer to Christ, not away from him. It truly can if we keep focused on Christ and view sport as a sacred vocation, not a secular avocation.

Luminous Mysteries

The Baptism of the Lord

"At that time Jesus came from Galilee to be baptized by John at the Jordan. John tried to prevent him and said, 'I need to be baptized by you, and you're coming to me?' But in answer Jesus said to him, 'Let it be, for now—it's fitting for us to fulfill all God's will in this way.'" (Matthew 3:13-15)

Jesus receives Baptism not because he needs it, but because we need it; he calls us to follow his lead. Consider the story of Jesus meeting the Samaritan woman at the well, which has strong connections to Baptism. (John 4:4-42) The Samaritan woman carries her heavy water jar to the well at noon, the hottest time of the day. No one came to the well at the sweltering noon hour because it was too difficult a task; the Samaritan woman performs this athletic feat in order to avoid being seen by anyone, for she is ashamed of her sinfulness. In the depths of her shame Jesus waits for her, to love her and to give her the "living water" which will create her anew. It took an athletic feat for her to find him.

At our Baptism we receive the living water and are joined to the saving death and resurrection of Christ. As such we become a new creation. We promise to renounce sin and to live according to faith in Christ. We must be faithful to these Baptismal promises in all we do in sport. Do we live and compete truly as the new creation we become in Baptism? Is there a noticeable difference in us as members of the body of Christ?

The Self-Revelation at Cana

When the wine runs out at the wedding in Cana, Mary approaches Jesus with the problem. Jesus is at first reluctant to do anything: "Jesus replied, 'What do you want from me, woman? My hour hasn't come yet.' His mother said to the servants, 'Do whatever he tells you.'" (John 2:4-5) Jesus calls for the six stone jars to be filled with water, and he miraculously changes the water into wine.

This story carries strong implications for Catholic athletes. It vividly illustrates a miracle of Jesus being performed through the cooperation of athletic people. The six stone jars each held between twenty and thirty gallons of water, so between 120 and

180 gallons of water needed to be drawn from a well and carried in these jars. This was a task requiring no small amount of athletic ability. Jesus took what began as an athletic accomplishment, blessed it, increased it, and used it for his ministry. Today he continues to work miracles of various degrees through his faithful followers who compete in athletics.

Mary played a key role in this event, as she continues to do today in the lives of her Son's disciples. Mary is truly our mother, watching over us, interceding for our needs, and assisting us in our journey. As she instructed the athletes at Cana to "Do whatever he tells you," she gives the same guidance to athletes today. Follow the Lord, and great things will be accomplished through us as his instruments.

The Proclamation of the Kingdom of God

"After John was arrested, Jesus came into Galilee proclaiming the good news of God and saying, 'The appointed time has come and the Kingdom of God is at hand; repent and believe in the good news!'" (Mark 1:14-15)

To repent and believe in the good news of the gospel are the promises we made at Baptism. The Kingdom of God is at hand everywhere, including the world of sports. Do we repent from whatever in our sport blinds us and keeps us away from the vision of God: pride, anger, dishonesty, laziness, selfishness, disrespect, a fear of truly living our faith? Do we honestly bring gospel values to all that we do?

The Transfiguration

"And it happened that as Moses and Elijah were leaving him, Peter said to Jesus, 'Master, it is good for us to be here; let's put up three dwellings, one for you, one for Moses, and one for Elijah'—he really didn't know what he was saying." (Luke 9:33) Peter is caught up in the glory and the grandeur of this incredible moment, and understandably so. Jesus' face changes appearance, his clothes become dazzling white, and he is conversing with Moses and Elijah, in proclamation that Jesus is the fulfillment of the law and the prophets. It is now time for the moment to end, but Peter wants to cling to it. His suggestion to build three dwellings is noble, but this glorious moment must end. Jesus and the disciples need to return to "the grind" of their daily life.

The life of an athlete is somewhat like this. There are peaks and there are valleys. The peaks are so glorious that the temptation to cling to them is strong. But the work must carry on.

Moments after winning the 2002 World Series, unabashed joy exuded in the Anaheim Angels' clubhouse as the team celebrated its first championship. Yet while most of the team celebrated, one member was spotted alone at his locker, a solemn look on his face. When asked what was wrong, he responded that now the hard part would begin. Now that the Angels were the champions, everyone would be after them the next season. The realization quickly set in that defending a championship is more difficult than winning one. The peak would soon become a necessary valley, and he must not cling to it.

As Christians we visit Mt. Tabor, but we also visit Calvary. Both are very sacred places to be.

The Institution of the Eucharist

> Jesus got up from the banquet and laid aside his cloak,
> and he took a towel and wrapped it around himself.
> Then he poured water into the washbasin and began
> to wash the disciples' feet and wipe them dry with the
> towel he'd wrapped around himself. When he came to
> Simon Peter, Peter said to him, "Lord, are *you* going to
> wash *my* feet?" Jesus answered and said to him, "What
> I'm doing you don't understand just now, but later you'll
> understand." Peter said to him, "You'll *never* wash my
> feet!" Jesus answered him, "Unless I wash you, you'll
> have no share in me." (John 13:4-8)

The night Jesus instituted the Eucharist, he gave an example of what it means to live the Eucharist. He was the leader of the team, and as such, there was no task so beneath him that he could not do it for the other members of the team. Washing feet was the job of a servant; Jesus showed that to be bread for others means to serve others, no matter what it takes.

Jesus' words to Peter, "Unless I wash you, you'll have no share in me," are in reference to Baptism, where—just like the Eucharist—Jesus will make his death and resurrection sacramentally present so we can be joined to them.

Sorrowful Mysteries

The Agony in the Garden

Jesus knows the difficult path that awaits him in the coming hours, and the pain, suffering, and ultimate sacrifice it will entail. In his humanity he first asks if this cup of suffering can pass him by, but then subjects himself totally to the will of the Father.

Jesus' passion and death are not for his own sake, but purely for the good of others. He will sacrifice himself for the life of all. Ironically his closest friends, benefactors of his saving death, have fallen asleep while Jesus agonizes over what he is about to do.

Our human nature often shrinks from the pain and sacrifice involved in using our gifts to glorify God. The divine image within each of us compels us to overcome the human temptation to avoid responsibility and to come through for those who are counting on us. An athlete calls upon the divine image within to respond to the challenges of competition. Joining our sports to Christ thus helps develop our lifelong vocation of allowing Jesus to restore us to the divine image.

The Scourging at the Pillar

Bound to a pillar, Jesus is forced to endure this agony, as the anger and hatred of others are unleashed upon him. He bears it with supreme courage and dignity.

Athletes can face hostility in competition—from opposing players, coaches, or fans. Christian athletes often face ridicule for expressing their faith in their sport. Jesus is the source of strength in enduring such trials. Opposition can make us stronger when we call upon Christ. "I'm able to do everything through the One who strengthens me." (Philippians 4:13) "Blessed are you when they insult you and persecute you and say every sort of evil thing against you on account of me; rejoice and be glad, because your reward will be great in heaven." (Matthew 5:11-12)

The Crowning with Thorns

The mockery and torture Jesus endures continues with the crown of thorns. Jesus is truly a king, but those who do not recognize this mock his claims. Ironically, while the crown of thorns was meant as an insult, it imaged the true crown of our true king, which we will share when we join him in his glory.

In his First Letter to the Corinthians, St. Paul wrote, "Everyone who competes in an athletic contest trains rigorously, but while they do it to win a perishable crown, we're competing for an imperishable crown." (1 Corinthians 9:25) The imperishable crown of Christ's glory comes with a price. Jesus has paid it, and calls us to join our sufferings to his as a participation in our salvation.

The Carrying of the Cross

"So they took Jesus in charge. And carrying the cross himself he went out to what was called 'the Place of the Skull,' in Hebrew, Golgotha." (John 19:16-17)

Once again, consider the tremendous athleticism that was involved in carrying the heavy cross through the streets of Jerusalem and up the hill to Calvary. Jesus' body, mind, spirit and will were united and totally focused on a goal so great that the ultimate sacrifice could be offered. Our salvation was achieved, in great part, through the athleticism of Christ. As athletes may we dedicate all that we do to his honor and glory.

The Crucifixion

"It was already about noon and darkness came over the whole land until about three o'clock, the sun having failed, while the sanctuary curtain was torn down the middle. Then Jesus called out with a loud voice, 'Father, into your hands I entrust my spirit!' And after saying this, he breathed his last." (Luke 23:44-46)

Jesus graciously "lost" to death on Good Friday, knowing that this was not to end in loss; three days later Jesus would defeat death. As discouraging as losing can be in athletic competition, the hope of a Christian is that any loss can be redeemed. Jesus having to "lose" to death on Good Friday was not something necessarily pleasing to God, for "God did not make death, nor does he rejoice in the destruction of the living. For he fashioned all things that they might have being." (Wisdom 1:13-14) But given the reality of death's entrance into the world through sin, God knew he had to submit Jesus to death to save us from it. Like death, loss in competition is something we don't want but is a reality of our imperfect state. Sometimes it is necessary to push us further to where we need to be. "Amen, amen, I say to you, if the grain of wheat that falls to the ground does not die, it remains alone, but if it dies, it bears much fruit." (John 12:24)

Glorious Mysteries

The Resurrection

"[Mary Magdalene and the other Mary] quickly left the tomb with fear and great joy and ran to tell the disciples." (Matthew 28:8) "On the first day of the week Mary Magdalene came to the tomb in the early morning while it was still dark, and she saw the stone, which had been taken away from the tomb. So she ran and came to Simon Peter and to the other disciple whom Jesus loved, and she said to them, 'They've taken the Lord out of the tomb and we don't know where they've put him!' So Peter and the other disciple went out and they went to the tomb. The two of them were running together, but the other disciple ran faster than Peter and came to the tomb first, and when he bent down he saw the linen cloths lying there, but he didn't go in." (John 20:1-5)

In both of these gospel accounts of Easter morning, running is an important detail. In Matthew's gospel the women run to tell the disciples about the resurrection. In the same way Simon Peter and the beloved disciple run to the tomb upon hearing the news, and it appears to be a race (with the detail about who ran faster and arrived first). The news is so great that their spirits command their bodies to move as fast as they can; indeed this first proclamation of the gospel required athleticism. Just as Mary's soul proclaimed the greatness of the Lord and her spirit rejoiced in God (Luke 1:46-47), her body was called to respond to this spiritual experience. So it is with athletics. The spirit moves the body to accomplish great things in and through Christ.

The Ascension

"Jesus said, 'When the Holy Spirit comes upon you you'll receive power and you'll be my witnesses in Jerusalem and in all Judea and Samaria, all the way to the end of the earth.' After he said these things he was taken up while they watched, and a cloud took him out of their sight." (Acts 1:8-9)

As the disciples look towards heaven their feet remain on earth, with plenty of work to do here. Jesus has left them with the promise of the Spirit, and that with the Spirit's help they will do great things. Indeed, all glory on earth points our attention to the glory of heaven. Earthly glory is merely a foretaste of what is to come. Any success, any glory won in athletics must be experienced as an image of what is yet to come, when God's will is accomplished in its fullness.

The Descent of the Holy Spirit

"Now when the day of Pentecost arrived they were all together in one place. Suddenly a sound like a violent rushing wind came from the sky and filled the whole house where they were staying. Tongues as if of fire appeared to them, parting and coming to rest on each of them, and they were all filled with the Holy Spirit and began to speak in different tongues according to how the Spirit inspired them to speak." (Acts 2:1-4)

As we read the New Testament we notice a dramatic difference in the behavior of the apostles before and after Pentecost. During the three years of Jesus' public ministry they appear cowardly, easily confused, argumentative, prideful, jealous, and seem to disappoint Jesus numerous times. Once they receive the Holy

Spirit their turnaround is astounding: they boldly go forth and proclaim the gospel, traveling to distant unknown lands, enduring persecution and risking their lives. That same Spirit is given to us in Baptism and Confirmation, and its gifts and fruits are plentiful and available in the athletic mission and in our apostolic vocation.

The Assumption of Mary

Mary is assumed body and soul into heaven, as she is sinless and full of grace. We who are sinful must experience physical death, but the Assumption of Mary is the promise of what we are to ultimately become. We do not become merely spiritual beings in heaven, for humanity is essentially body and soul united, now and forever. Just as Jesus rose with a glorified body, and Mary was assumed with a body already in a state of glory because of her lack of sin, we will receive glorified bodies in eternity. What a powerful reminder of the responsibility to care for the bodies we live in now, and the respect they are due as temples of the Holy Spirit.

Mary is Crowned Queen of Heaven and Earth

The joyful mysteries begin with Mary; the glorious mysteries culminate with her. Mary who is the new Eve, bringing forth the Savior who conquered sin and death brought about through the first Eve, is now the Queen of Heaven and Earth, the culmination of a life lived totally for God. This points us to her Son, the alpha and the omega, the beginning and the end. May all our endeavors as athletes, beginning through end, glorify God.

Questions for Individual Reflection or Group Discussion

Compare your experience of personal prayer with your experience of praying with and for others. Is there a correlation with your prayer time with Mary?

Are there certain mysteries of the Rosary that touch you in a special way?

CHAPTER FIVE

No Pain, No Gain

Every athlete is familiar with this expression, and understands what it means. Athletes have to strengthen their bodies, sharpen their minds, and deepen their will to do what it takes to succeed.

It all comes with a price. Muscles get sore when they're exercised, pushed to do something they may not be used to. The body gets tired, often before it is allowed to shut down and rest. Sports are mentally demanding, requiring the ability to make split-second decisions, to outsmart an opponent, to anticipate, to react. The will is surely tested, especially in the face of exhaustion, to keep going when rest or other activities are tempting.

"No pain, no gain" is easy to understand—accepting it is another matter. The spirit ultimately drives the body; how one accepts the more painful demands of sport determines whether the spirit will be positive or negative.

Life in the Eucharist has the same demands. Comfort zones are not places of great spiritual growth. Disciples are called to push beyond the familiar, to exercise virtues they may not be used to developing, to resist the temptation to abandon the mission when they are weary and the road ahead seems too long.

When we feed on the body of Christ that suffered for us—and are joined to that suffering body—suffering is necessarily part of the journey. Jesus' suffering heals us from our condition as sinners separated from God. Like any physical disease or injury, if we want to be healed of what ails us, we must accept any suffering that comes with the cure. Since our healing is in Jesus' wounds, we must enter them to be healed.

Jesus teaches "No pain, no gain," but in somewhat different words: "Whoever would be my disciple must deny himself. He must take up his cross and follow me." (Matthew 16:24)

So what does it mean to take up a cross? Does any kind of suffering constitute a cross, or must suffering be explicitly in the pursuit of the Kingdom of God?

People have various interpretations of what it means to take up a cross. Some would propose that not all suffering is necessarily a cross, because a cross must be freely chosen. Since Jesus freely chose to carry his cross for us, some would hold that only sufferings that we deliberately choose should be rightly regarded as crosses. They would not consider illness, for example, or the death of a loved one, or being fired from one's job to be crosses, since nobody chooses any of those things.

It is true there is a lot of suffering in our life that we do not choose. (Suffering sometimes comes as a result of things we choose to do, but we do not usually choose to suffer.) Yet once we are suffering, we do have a choice of what to do about it. We can choose to be angry, feel sorry for ourselves, or bemoan the apparent injustice of something terrible happening to good people like us. Or we can choose to embrace the suffering as an opportunity to join ourselves to the sufferings of Christ. The latter is choosing to take up a cross, and it can be done whether the suffering itself was chosen or not.

As we discussed in Chapter One, all suffering can become a participation in the redemptive work of Christ if we freely choose to join it to his suffering as members of his body. Suffering experienced in sports is pain endured in a noble cause, and is worthy to be joined to Christ's cross.

Taking up a cross means placing our suffering on the cross of Christ—not each of us carrying crosses individually, but collectively sharing the burden of Jesus' cross which he took upon himself for all of us. In doing so we are actually lightening the burden of the entire body, for we are all truly carrying one cross, with Jesus carrying the brunt of the load.

When contemplating our suffering, it is important to remember its root cause—sin. Not that all of our personal suffering is necessarily "inflicted" upon us by God for our personal sins. ("You lied to your coach, so you're getting the flu today.") Suffering exists in general because sin exists in general. God created the world in perfect harmony, and intended for us to live forever in happy union with him. When our first ancestors allowed sin into the world it forever disrupted the original harmony; a "Pandora's Box" was opened that cannot be completely closed. Sin brought both suffering and death into the world, which God never wanted for us in the first place. They were the natural consequences of humanity severing the lifeline to our Creator.

Since sin is the root cause of suffering and death, it took Jesus' suffering and death to save us from sin. While suffering and death still exist because sin still exists—and we must deal with both realities—Jesus saved us from the ultimate consequence of sin, which is eternal suffering and death.

God both predicted suffering as a permanent part of the human condition and promised the coming of a savior in the Garden of Eden. Speaking to the serpent who brought temptation into the world, God said: "I will put enmity between you and the woman, and between your offspring and hers; he will strike at your head, while you strike at his heel." (Genesis 3:15) The serpent's offspring represent evil and all who are drawn to it. Evil will always strike at the heel of the woman's offspring, causing pain and suffering. But an offspring of the woman will one day strike at the *head* of the serpent—conquering it once and for all. (This is why Mary is often depicted in Catholic art stepping on a snake. Mary is the "New Eve," pinning down the serpent so her Son can strike at its head.)

In joining our suffering to that of Jesus, we can take comfort in the fact that Jesus entered into ours, and still does. During his time on earth Jesus experienced human pain. His spirit groaned and he wept at the death of his friend Lazarus. He knew the pain of rejection, persecution, and being disappointed by loved ones. We are told he had compassion on the crowds who were like sheep without a shepherd. Compassion means "suffer with." Jesus agonized in the garden the night before his death, and endured the intense physical and spiritual pain of his passion and death.

There is no pain in our lives that Jesus cannot identify with and share, and place on his cross so that we don't have to carry it by ourselves. Stated a bit more positively: "With pain, there is gain."

Question for Individual Reflection or Group Discussion

Read Psalm 22, the opening of which Jesus proclaimed from the cross: "My God, my God, why have you abandoned me?" Notice how the first twenty-two verses are a lamentation over suffering; yet beginning with verse 23 it becomes a song of praise to God, confident in his promise of deliverance. Meditate upon suffering in your own life with this psalm in its entirety, which Jesus quoted on the cross.

CHAPTER SIX

Through the Seasons of the Liturgical Year

In his bestselling book *Bunts*, George F. Will writes that he divides the year not into four seasons, but two: baseball season, and "The Void." Indeed, from the final out of the World Series to the first pitch of Opening Day, "The Void" is an annual desert journey for those to whom baseball is the center of their sports world. Yet "The Void" is a necessary destination for anyone looking to grow. Fasting from the game for a period of time, baseball teams and fans have the chance to reflect upon the past and prepare for the future. "The Void" is an opportunity to examine the prior season's failures, uproot their causes, and plan for success in the coming campaign. The dawn of a new season offers hope, a new beginning, a chance to start again with the past forgiven yet valuable lessons learned.

For Catholic baseball devotees, it is a blessing that Opening Day usually coincides with the end of Lent and the start of the Easter season. Lent is our "Void," when we journey through a spiritual desert in anticipation of the celebration of Christ's resurrection. It is a time to scrutinize our lives and uproot what is weak, so that when Jesus comes to raise us to the Father we may be made worthy of the promise given to us at our Baptism, expressed in the blessing of the water: "May all who are buried with Christ in the death of Baptism rise also with him to newness of life." Easter is our "Opening Day," when Jesus opened not only his tomb but ours as well, and called us to journey with him from despair to hope, from sorrow to joy, from darkness to light, from death to life. To properly prepare for that celebration, we need the time "The Void" offers.

All sports follow a seasonal calendar; the life of an athlete requires a cycle to balance the various activities necessary for success: a time to train, a time to practice, a time to compete, a time to crown champions, a time to evaluate, a time to plan, a time to rest. The life of Eucharistic people follows a cycle as well, called the liturgical calendar or the liturgical year. We feed on the Eucharist year round. But how we celebrate Eucharist varies throughout the year. We need to focus our attention on the extraordinary events that brought us salvation: the birth of Jesus, his death and resurrection, his ascension into heaven and his sending of the Holy Spirit upon the Church. We also need to reflect on his presence and movement in our everyday lives. The Church year is divided into various seasons to help us accomplish all of this. We have no "off-season" as disciples of Jesus; however, we do have grander and more subdued times of worship to help us maintain our balance.

Sports begin with a time to train and prepare for competition. The liturgical year begins with Advent, the roughly four-week period prior to Christmas. Our focus during Advent is not only preparing to celebrate Christ's first coming to the world with his birth at Bethlehem, but preparing for his second coming as well, whenever that may be. John the Baptist is a central figure in this season, calling us to repent of our sins and prepare the way of the Lord. Advent focuses our attention on the need to be always vigilant, to train in the exercise of Christian virtue, and to always be ready for the coming of Christ.

Christmas comes next, when we remember the remarkable event where God and humanity meet as one, his revelation is fulfilled, and we begin our eternal union with God. As such, Christmas is very much about Eucharist.

Already with the birth of the Savior there are indications of Jesus' Eucharistic mission and its highly physical nature. Bethlehem, the city God chose for his birth, is Hebrew for "House of Bread." The swaddling clothes in which Jesus is wrapped foreshadow the burial shroud that will hold his body between his death and resurrection. Mary lays the newborn king in a manger—a feeding trough—as a sign of his ultimate mission to be food for the world. He is born in a borrowed cave, just as he will be buried in a borrowed cave.

At Christmas we are greeted with a unique athletic image from Scripture. The first reading for Mass during the day on Christmas begins: "How beautiful upon the mountains are the feet of him who brings glad tidings." (Isaiah 52:7) Feet may not be normally considered a "beautiful" part of our body. But in the Christian tradition feet are very significant. Jesus journeyed by foot to perform his ministry. His feet were anointed in preparation for his passion. Jesus commanded the disciples to go forth without sandals or walking sticks—to rely on the endurance of their bare feet. Jesus washed the feet of the apostles at the Last Supper as an example of service. Jesus walked to Calvary, and had his feet nailed to the cross.

Feet are crucial to athletic competition and to the Christian mission. We are reminded at Christmas that they are truly beautiful when used to spread the gospel!

Next comes a brief period of "ordinary time," between the conclusion of the Christmas season and Ash Wednesday, the start of Lent. Ordinary time then resumes after Pentecost, and continues until the first Sunday of Advent begins a new year.

Ordinary time comprises the largest portion of the Church year. A brief way to define it is whenever we are not celebrating one of the major feasts or seasons: Advent, Christmas, Lent, Easter, or Pentecost. But its purpose is to truly focus our attention on the "ordinary times" of our lives, and how God is present and working in everyday situations. While it may be considered somewhat of a liturgical "down time," it is definitely not an off-season. Quite the opposite, since ordinary time makes up the major part of the Church year, it is a time to reflect upon the movements of God during the majority of our "ordinary life."

"The Void" of Lent begins with Ash Wednesday and continues through the Wednesday of Holy Week. It includes the physical disciplines of fasting on Ash Wednesday and Good Friday, and abstaining from meat on Fridays. Like our reflection on Eucharistic adoration in Chapter Three indicated, our physical hunger can help gauge our longing for the risen Jesus we celebrate at Easter.

Lent concludes with the Sacred Triduum, the three holiest days of the year. We commemorate the institution of the Eucharist on Holy Thursday, Jesus' passion and death on Good Friday, and the glory of the resurrection at the Easter Vigil. These three days are rich in physical signs that engage our bodily senses.

Feet are washed at the Mass of the Lord's Supper on Holy Thursday; following the liturgy the Blessed Sacrament is carried in solemn procession with a humeral veil to a chapel of repose separate from the worship space for adoration.

On Good Friday the church building is barren: there are no flowers, no altar cloth, statues and other images are usually covered, the tabernacle is empty as a stark reminder that this is the day Jesus entered death. The priest begins the Good Friday liturgy with the most profound physical gesture of worship—he lays prostrate in front of the altar. We come forward to venerate a cross with a kiss, a bow, or other physical gesture of reverence. This is the only day of the year that bread and wine are not consecrated to become Eucharist, to emphasize Jesus' death; we receive Eucharist that was consecrated at the Holy Thursday Mass.

The Easter Vigil begins in darkness, a sign of the darkness of sin from which we need to be saved. The darkness is pierced by the light of the newly blessed Paschal Candle, a sign of the light of Christ piercing our darkness and leading us out. The faithful take the light of Christ from the Paschal Candle with smaller candles. As more people accept the light of Christ, the darkness is dispelled. We witness Baptisms and Confirmations of people entering the Church, and join them at the table of the Eucharist. It is truly the high point of the liturgical year.

The Easter season continues for seven more weeks. We celebrate Jesus' ascension into heaven, and conclude the season with Pentecost. This is when Jesus sent the Holy Spirit over the apostles, empowering them to go forth and spread the gospel. Pentecost is sometimes called the "birthday of the Church," and presents us with a remarkable image of a team. Jesus had already assembled the players, but it was through their union in the Eucharist and their empowerment with the Holy Spirit that they became a team. This is confirmed by the miracle of people from many nations hearing the apostles speak in their own languages, and the extraordinary courage shown by the apostles, courage that had been conspicuously absent prior to Pentecost.

We began this chapter with a reflection on Lent and Easter. Since Easter is the high point of the liturgical year, and our "Opening Day," we'll return there for our conclusion.

Athletes and fans know well the liberation of letting go of the failures of past seasons and embarking upon a fresh campaign on Opening Day. While we can readily relinquish our emotional ties to the past wounds of sports, doing the same in our spiritual lives sometimes proves much more challenging.

Consider the story of "Doubting Thomas." When the news of Christ's resurrection reached the apostles, Thomas refused to believe until he could examine the wounds in the Lord's hands, feet and side. When Jesus appeared and offered him the chance to do just that, Thomas proclaimed, "My Lord and my God." Jesus said to him, "Have you come to believe because you have seen me? Blessed are those who have not seen and have believed." (John 20:29) Thomas' faith depended on seeing and touching Jesus' wounds. Yet Jesus invited Thomas to move to a deeper stage of relationship. He bid Thomas not to dwell on the wounds of the past, but to move beyond them into a new tomorrow, a brighter future where wounds are healed and life is restored.

Easter reminds us to leave wounds of the past behind us, for

Jesus has come to heal them and lead us past them into a glorious future where anything is possible with God. In union with Christ, together as his body, we journey as a team through Opening Day to the ultimate post-season promise: "God's dwelling is with the human race. He will dwell with them and they will be his people and God himself will always be with them. He will wipe every tear from their eyes, and there shall be no more death or mourning, wailing or pain, for the old order has passed away." (Revelation 21:3-4)

Alleluia!

Question for Individual Reflection or Group Discussion

Read Ecclesiastes 3:1-8. Reflect on how the various times in our lives for both physical and spiritual activities strengthen us as both athletes and Eucharistic people.

CHAPTER SEVEN

Run to Win—But Should We Pray to Win?

Baseball managing legend Tommy Lasorda once joked, "I never pray that we win—I pray that we don't lose." With prayer becoming more openly expressed in athletic activities the question is inevitable: is it proper to pray for victory? Catholics, other Christians, and athletes of various religions face this question at some point. How do we address it, and what are some of the underlying spiritual principles in prayers offered for success in sports?

A good starting point is to ponder these words of Jesus: "Everyone who exalts himself will be humbled, and whoever humbles himself will be exalted." (Luke 14:11; also 18:14) This message is so important that Jesus issued it not just once, but in two separate incidents in the Gospel accounts. To the guests choosing places of honor at a banquet, Jesus advised taking the lowest seats, and waiting for the host to invite them to a higher position. In the parable of the Pharisee and the tax collector, Jesus championed the sinner who humbly admitted his failings and prayed for forgiveness, over the Pharisee who praised his own virtue. In both instances Christ's message is clear: exaltation is not ours to seek or to bestow—it is granted by the Father through our humility in prayer, word and action.

Praying for victory simply for the satisfaction and glory it brings would seem contrary to Christ's teaching. If the object of such prayer is merely to seek our own glorification, then we need to look no further than the Savior's words noted above for resolution. But success in athletics can have broader ramifications; it can open doors to various avenues for God's grace, which should be taken into account when discerning the propriety of praying to win.

For Christian athletes who seek to spread the Good News of Christ, success in sports means higher visibility and a larger stage from which to evangelize. Victory in sports, especially when it comes in a dramatic fashion or against steep odds, has an inspiring quality that can arouse others to apply the lessons learned to their own life. Any victory gained through hard work, preparation, discipline and effective teamwork has lessons to offer far beyond the sports world.

While these by-products of athletic success have positive implications for Christian mission, does it still justify praying for victory? Or should prayer humbly ask God to help us to do our best, leaving the outcome to his providential care? Perhaps a healthy mix of both is the right approach.

As in everything in our lives, the Lord's example is the best to follow. On the night before his death, Jesus prayed, "Father, if you are willing, take this cup away from me; still, not my will but yours be done." (Luke 22:42) Jesus honestly expresses to the Father his human desires; but ultimately his divine nature prevails and he prays that God's will be done. In the same way God wants us to honestly tell him our real desires, whether or not they are truly the best for us. God wants us to openly share our wants with him because only he can properly sort them out, and help us learn what we should really pursue.

Yet while we honestly tell him what our will may be, God calls us to accept *his* will, whether or not it coincides with our wants. If we desperately want victory we should tell that to God, who understands our hearts better than we do, and knows if our motives are pure or tainted by sin. God can then take our prayer and answer us with the wisdom and counsel we truly need. Maybe victory is the best thing for us; maybe God wants us—or we need—to lose. In either event, using our God-given talents to the best of our ability and striving to win while submitting in true humility to God's will is the only proper path.

The issue of praying for victory begs two fundamental questions: What is Christian humility, and what is the purpose of prayer?

Humility

Humility is an honest acknowledgment of all that we are, truly recognizing our weaknesses as well as our strengths. But above all humility is the recognition that God is all-powerful and all knowing—and we are not—and that all of our accomplishments are ultimately God's work being performed through us as his instruments.

The prophet Jeremiah beautifully expressed the essence of humility:

Thus says the Lord:
Let not the wise man glory in his wisdom,
nor the strong man glory in his strength,
nor the rich man glory in his riches;
But rather, let him who glories, glory in this,
that in his prudence he knows me,
Knows that I, the Lord, bring about kindness,
justice and uprightness on the earth;
For with such I am pleased, says the Lord.
(Jeremiah 9:22-23)

All our talents come from God. We work with them through our own effort, but ultimately all our accomplishments flow from God and are for his greater glory. Because everything is really God's work, God can accomplish great things not only through our strengths, but especially through our weaknesses. When we admit where we are weak and invite God to work through those areas where we cannot, great things can happen.

St. Paul's writings are rich with the power of acknowledging our weakness:

[The Lord] told me, "My grace is enough for you, for my power is made perfect in your weakness." Therefore I'm all the more pleased to boast of my weaknesses, so that Christ's power may dwell with me. For this reason I delight in weakness, insults, hardships, persecution, and difficulties for Christ's sake, for when I'm weak, that's when I'm strong. (2 Corinthians 12:9-10)

For by grace you have been saved through faith; and this was God's gift, it didn't come from you, not from your own efforts, so that no one would be able to boast. For we are his handiwork, created in Christ Jesus for the purpose of carrying out those good works for which God prepared us beforehand, so that we might lead our lives in the performance of good works. (Ephesians 2:8-10)

Far be it for me to boast of anything but the cross of Christ. (Galatians 6:14)

Whoever boasts should boast in the Lord, for the one whom the Lord commends is the one who's approved, not the one who commends himself. (2 Corinthians 10:17)

Perhaps St. Paul best sums up humility in this passage from his Letter to the Philippians:

If life in Christ provides any encouragement, any comfort in love, any sharing in the Spirit, any affection and compassion, then complete my joy by being of one mind, sharing the same love, being united in spirit, and thinking as one. Do nothing out of selfishness or a desire to boast; instead, in a spirit of humility toward one another, regard others as better than yourselves. Each of you should look out for the rights of others, rather than looking after your own rights. Have the same outlook among you that Christ Jesus had,

Who, though he was in the form of God,
did not consider equality with God
something to hold on to.
Instead, he emptied himself and took on
the form of a slave,
born in human likeness,
and to all appearances a man.
He humbled himself and became obedient,
even unto death, death on a cross.
For this reason God exalted him
and gave him a name above every
other name,
So that at the name of Jesus every knee shall bend,
In the heavens, on earth, and below the earth,
And every tongue proclaim to the glory
of God the Father,
that Jesus Christ is Lord.
(Philippians 2:1-11)

The Purpose of Prayer

The issue of praying for victory also begs the question: What is the purpose of prayer, and how do we gauge its success?

There is a story about two Catholic baseball managers who spotted each other at Mass one Sunday morning, on a day their teams would oppose each other later in the afternoon. After Mass one of the managers watched the other walk over to a stand of vigil lights. He lit a candle, knelt down in prayer, and then got up and went on his way. After watching this, the other manager got up, walked over to the vigil lights, knelt down in prayer, and extinguished the other's candle.

Whether or not the story is true, it illustrates an important point. Whichever team won, did it mean their manager's prayer was better? Did God take sides between these two men who were both praying for the same outcome? Or is there more to our prayers and God's answers to them?

Sometimes we tend to think of prayer as a drive-thru window where we place our order for what we would like God to give us. When we get to the window we sometimes find (as we do in real drive-thru windows) that what we are handed is not what we "ordered." A drive-thru approach to prayer is even more frustrating than the clerk who gives a salad when we asked for a burger—though that outcome is analogous to how God often answers our prayers.

While God wants us to ask him for things, receiving what we ask for is not the goal of prayer. Asking God for what we need (as opposed to what we want) verifies our dependence upon him, and keeps our relationship with God in the proper order. But God will give us what is best for us, regardless of what we ask him for, and in doing so he does his part to strengthen his relationship with us. Whether or not the relationship is fully strengthened depends upon our response—whether we accept our dependence upon him and his will for us, or if we resist.

Jesus vividly described the importance of asking God for our needs. When the disciples asked him how they should pray, Jesus gave them the Lord's Prayer. He then elaborated:

If any of you had a friend and you went to him at midnight and said to him, "Friend, lend me three loaves— my friend has arrived on a journey to me and I haven't a thing to set before him," would he answer from inside, "Don't bother me! The door's already locked and my children are with me in the bed; I can't get up and give you anything." I tell you, even if he doesn't get up and give you something because he's your friend, he'll get up and give you whatever you need out of a sense of shame. And to you I say,

Ask! and it shall be given to you;

Seek! and you shall find;

Knock! and it shall be opened to you.

For everyone who asks, receives;

And whoever seeks will find;

And to those who knock it shall be opened.

But is there a father among you who,

if his son asks for a fish,

instead of a fish will hand him a snake?

Or if he asks for an egg,

will hand him a scorpion?

So if you who are evil know how

to give good gifts to your children,

All the more will the Father from heaven

give the Holy Spirit to those who ask him! (Luke 11:5-13)

By contrasting God with the images of the friend and the father, Jesus teaches that God will provide everything we need when we ask him in sincerity of heart. If human beings know how to give, so much more does God.

But he also teaches that we will be given what we *need*, which is not always what we *want*. One of the goals of the Christian life is to have our wills transformed into God's so that what we ultimately want is our basic needs to be met.

"Ask! and it shall be given to you" is not to be confused with "God will give you anything you ask for." "Seek! and you shall find" implies that we cannot expect to be handed everything. God calls us to *search* for him, and in doing so grow into deeper union with him. In the conclusion of the story of the father who provides for his children's needs, Jesus reminds us of our ultimate need: "All the more will the Father from heaven give the Holy Spirit to those who ask him!"

The gifts of the Holy Spirit are wisdom, understanding, counsel, strength, knowledge, piety, and fear of the Lord. The fruits of the Holy Spirit are love, joy, peace, patience, kindness, goodness, faith, gentleness, and self-control. With the gifts and fruits of the Holy Spirit we have everything we need.

Questions for Individual Reflection or Group Discussion

Read the passages from Scripture where we derive the gifts of the Holy Spirit—Isaiah 11:1-9—and the fruits of the Holy Spirit—Galatians 5:16-26—and reflect upon them.

How do you pray regarding your participation in sports? How does it fit into the rest of your prayer life?

How do you spiritually handle both victory and defeat?

CHAPTER EIGHT

Body Image

We noted in Chapter One that the body of Christ is not merely an image—it is our central reality. Yet the body as an image does have much to say about our life in the Eucharist. This chapter will explore that image as it has been developed in our Catholic tradition.

This famous passage from St. Paul's First Letter to the Corinthians presents the human body as an image for the body of Christ, which has many implications for Catholic athletes:

> For the body isn't one member—it's made up of many members. If the foot should say, "I'm not a hand, so I'm not part of the body," it would still be part of the body for all that, and if the ear should say, "I'm not the eye, so I'm not part of the body," it would still be part of the body for all that. If the whole body were an eye, how could it hear? If the whole body were an ear, how could it smell? But as it is, God arranged the members of the body—each one of them—as he wished them

to be. If they were all just one member, what sort of body would that be? As it is, though, there are many members, but one body. The eye can't tell the hand, "I have no need of you," nor can the head tell the feet, "I have no need of you." On the contrary, the members of the body which seem the weakest are much more necessary, the members of the body which seem less honorable are the ones we grant the most honor to, and our private parts we treat with more modesty, whereas there's no need to present our more presentable parts that way. But God has formed the body in such a way as to give greater honor to the members which lack it, so that there will be no discord in the body and the members will feel the same concern for one another. If one member suffers, all the members suffer; if one member is honored, all the members rejoice. (1 Corinthians 12:14-26)

The importance of teamwork is an obvious lesson. A team is made up of individual members with different roles, but it functions as a group to pursue a common goal while also trying to defeat an opponent. Everyone has individual strengths, but they are not enough to achieve victory, for everyone has individual weaknesses as well. When teammates join together the weaknesses of one are complemented by the strengths of another, and the team accomplishes what no one on their own could possibly do.

The Christian life is the same. We have goals set before us—both individually and as a community—which are difficult to obtain because there is always an opponent working against us who does not want us to win. We all have individual strengths and weaknesses, but we only progress when we pool all of our efforts. Each and every member of the body is crucial to success. We win or lose as one body.

While the communal aspect of teamwork may be obvious, it can be easily overlooked when individual accomplishments are given too much emphasis, for good or for bad. Professional sports offer many examples. Two from the history of the World Series are notable.

Bill Mazeroski is often remembered as "winning" the 1960 World Series for the Pittsburgh Pirates with a home run in the bottom of the ninth inning of game seven, breaking a tie with the New York Yankees. Yet had his teammates not worked together to score the other runs (and prevented the Yankees from scoring more) Mazeroski never would have had that moment. If he and his teammates had not won three previous games, they would not have been in a position to win the series. If the team had not allowed the Yankees to win three games, there would not have even been a game seven!

On the negative side, Bill Buckner is often remembered as "losing" the 1986 World Series for the Boston Red Sox by letting a ground ball roll through his legs at first base—allowing the New York Mets to tie and eventually win the World Series—when the Red Sox were one strike away from winning. Again, if the Red Sox as a team had been able to score a few more runs that night, or had kept the Mets from scoring more, or had the Red Sox won another game earlier in the series, Buckner would never have been in that position in the first place.

Games are won or lost by *teams*, not by individuals. While

one player's actions may seem to win or lose a game, the pivotal situation was provided by the entire team. This concept is central to Christianity. None of us comes to God alone. God created us in the community of the Church, and draws us to himself through Jesus Christ in community, the Church. As St. Paul writes, "If one member suffers, all the members suffer; if one member is honored, all the members rejoice."

St. Paul also writes, "The members of the body which seem the weakest are much more necessary, the members of the body which seem less honorable are the ones we grant the most honor to…. God has formed the body in such a way as to give greater honor to the members which lack it, so that there will be no discord in the body and the members will feel the same concern for one another."

He elaborated on this point earlier in his First Letter to the Corinthians:

Consider the fact that *you* were called. Not many of you were wise according to the flesh, nor powerful or well-born, but God chose the foolish things of the world to shame those who are wise, the weak of the world to shame the strong; God chose the base-born and contemptible of the world, things that are nothing, to shame what is, so that the flesh would have nothing to boast of before God. Through God you are in Christ Jesus, and through God Christ became our wisdom, righteousness, sanctification, and redemption, so that as it is written, "Whoever boasts, let him boast in the Lord." (1 Corinthians 1:26-31)

The body as an image offers other lessons for the life of a disciple, especially the athletic quality of the body. Success in athletics requires discipline, strengthening, proper nourishment, and good decision-making. The Christian life is no different. Like an athlete in training, a Christian is often tempted to abandon his or her "workout routine" for other activities that may seem more enticing at the moment. The Christian life is demanding—success requires strength to endure to the end. Decision-making is crucial to the Christian, for free will can either lead to true freedom or slavery to sin. Without the proper nourishment—the body and blood of Christ—Christians have no life in them.

From Jesus' body on the cross comes a profound image of the Church and her sacraments. In the Gospel of John we read: "The soldiers came and broke the legs of the first one and then of the other who had been crucified with him, but when they came to Jesus and saw that he'd already died they didn't break his legs, but instead, one of the soldiers stabbed him in the side with a spear, and at once blood and water came out." (John 19: 32-34) This is an image of the sacramental life of the Church being born from Jesus' death. The water represents Baptism, the blood signifies the Eucharist. These are two sacramental ways Jesus established though his Church to join us sacramentally to his saving death, to make it truly present again so we can be truly joined to it. Since we have reflected quite a bit on Eucharist, we'll take this opportunity to look at Baptism.

The New Testament is clear that our Baptism is a participation in the death of Jesus. The Lord himself uses the term to refer to his death: "Jesus said [to the disciples], 'Can you drink the cup I am drinking, or be baptized with the baptism with which I am being baptized?' 'We can,' they said. But Jesus said to them, 'The cup I am drinking you will drink; and with the baptism with which I am being baptized, you will be baptized.'" (Mark 10: 38-39) And again: "I have a baptism to be baptized with, and how apprehensive I am until it is accomplished!" (Luke 12:50) St. Paul wrote to the Romans: "Don't you know that those of us who were baptized into Christ Jesus were baptized into his death? Therefore, we were buried with him through our baptism into his death, so that just as Christ was raised from the dead by the Father's glory we too might be able to lead a new life." (Romans 6:3-4)

Baptism gives a physical experience of that true union with Jesus' death and resurrection; one method in particular gives a profound physical experience. While one may be baptized with a pouring of water over the head, full immersion in water is the fullest sign of the reality that is taking place. Like a diver plunging into water, a person being baptized by immersion needs to hold their breath. The cessation of breath symbolizes death. Being totally surrounded by water and stopping their breathing is a sign to the baptized person that they are at that moment truly entering into the death of Jesus. Buried in the baptismal water, they are buried with Jesus in his tomb. Rising from the water and breathing again is a sign of the new life into which they have truly just been born.

The ritual of Baptism thus carries strong athletic overtones (including the anointing with oil discussed in Chapter One), and joins us to the death and resurrection of Christ that was accomplished in great part through Jesus' athleticism.

One more passage from St. Paul presents athletic images to describe life in the Eucharist, and provides a fitting reflection for all Catholic athletes:

Become strong through the Lord's power and might. Put on God's armor so you'll be able to stand up against the schemes of the Devil, for we're not engaged in a struggle with mere flesh and blood—we're fighting against the rulers and powers, against the cosmic powers of this dark world, against the spiritual forces of evil in the heavens. Therefore, take up God's armor so you'll be able to oppose them on the day of evil and, by doing everything in your power, to remain standing. So stand firm! Gird your loins with truth and put on the breastplate of righteousness! Put on your feet the boots of preparedness for the good news of peace! And along with all this take up the shield of the faith, with which you'll be able to extinguish all the flaming arrows of the Evil One. Take the helmet of salvation and the sword of the Spirit, which is the word of God. (Ephesians 6:10-17)

Questions for Individual Reflection or Group Discussion

What part do you play in the body of Christ? How does your participation in sports strengthen this image?

Have you experienced times when a member of a team has been singled out as either a "hero" or a "goat"? Have you experienced times outside of sports when something similar has happened? How can you witness in such situations as a member of the body of Christ?

CHAPTER NINE

A Mentor for Catholic Athletes

Catholics have long treasured the Communion of Saints as patrons, role models, mentors and intercessors. In 1990 Pope John Paul II beatified a young man with a love for sports and a passion for the Eucharist and the life that flows from it. His name is Blessed Pier Giorgio Frassati, and Catholic athletes would do well to become acquainted with his brief but remarkable earthly life, and to grow in relationship with him as a heavenly mentor and intercessor. We'll conclude our reflection on living the Eucharist through sports with an introduction to this inspiring young man.

Pier Giorgio Frassati was born in Turin, Italy, on April 6, 1901, to a well-known and powerful political family. His father was the founder and publisher of an influential newspaper, and served as a senator and Italy's ambassador to Germany. Growing up in northwest Italy in the shadow of the Alps, Pier Giorgio fell in love with the mountains and the athletic activities to be enjoyed there: hiking, skiing and horseback riding were among his favorite pastimes.

But his true athletic passion was mountain climbing. Pier

Giorgio was a member of the Italian Alpine Club, and climbed to the peaks of the Gran Tournalin, the Grivola in the Val d' Aosta, the Mon Viso, the Ciamarella, and the Bessanese—each with an altitude over 3300 meters. He also climbed many other lower mountain peaks.

His motto was: "Verso l' alto," which means, "Toward the top." But these words described far more than Frassati's passion for mountain climbing—they speak of his ultimate goal of seeking God and striving for heaven.

Pier Giorgio used his sporting activities as a vehicle to help him and his companions reach this goal. "I left my heart on the mountain peaks and I hope to retrieve it this summer when I climb Mont Blanc," he wrote to a friend. "If my studies permitted, I would spend whole days on the mountain, exploring in that pure atmosphere the magnificence of God."

Frassati would organize mountain climbing expeditions and use them as opportunities for evangelization. He would unashamedly share his love for Christ with his companions, and encourage them to share details of their spiritual lives. Outings would include Scripture readings, the Rosary, and hikes to the nearest church to attend Mass. Frassati's actions while climbing often revealed the selfless disciple he truly was, as he would take others' burdens upon himself. Sometimes he would pretend that his feet hurt or that he needed to stop, so as not to embarrass those who really needed to rest. Or he would make several trips up and down the mountain carrying items in order to lighten the backpacks of those who were weaker.

Pier Giorgio was a man of intense prayer and apostolic action. At a young age he joined the Marian Sodality and the

Apostleship of Prayer, and was given permission to receive daily Communion, a rarity at the time. At age seventeen he joined the St. Vincent de Paul Society, and devoted much of his time to service of the poor, sick, orphaned, and servicemen returning home from World War I. He joined the Federation of Italian Catholic University Students, where Pope John Paul II said "he found the true gymnasium of his Christian training and the right fields of his apostolate." Frassati also became active with the Peoples Party, an organization that promoted Catholic social teachings based on Pope Leo XIII's encyclical *Rerum Novarum.* In 1922 Frassati joined the Third Order of St. Dominic (Lay Dominicans) where he found a further outlet for his Eucharistic adoration and apostolic zeal.

His deep faith led Pier Giorgio to political activism, which at times forced him to literally fight to defend the faith, especially against the threat of Fascism that was on the rise at the time in Italy. Once while participating in a Church-organized demonstration in Rome he and some other youths were attacked by police, who knocked down a banner some of them had been holding. Frassati retrieved the banner and held it aloft, using the pole to fend off blows by the police. When he was arrested he refused special treatment available to him because of his father's political position, choosing to stay with the other students.

On another occasion Fascists invaded his family's home to attack Pier Giorgio and his father. He beat them off single-handedly and chased them down the street.

Yet despite his strong physical nature, Pier Giorgio was gentle at heart. His works of mercy were plentiful, selfless, and often hidden.

For example:

As a young boy he gave his shoes to another boy who had none, when the poor boy's mother came begging at the Frassati home.

He would give his bus fare away to help the poor, and then run home to be on time for meals.

When he graduated his father gave him the choice of money or a car as a gift; he chose the money and gave it to the poor.

He would often forgo vacations with his family, saying, "If everybody leaves Turin, who will take care of the poor?"

While his father served as ambassador to Germany, a reporter for a German newspaper observed: "One night in Berlin, with the temperature at twelve degrees below zero, he gave his coat to a poor old man shivering with cold. His father scolded him and he replied simply and matter-of-factly, 'But you see, Papa, it was cold.'"

He rented a room for a poor old woman who had been evicted from her apartment.

He supported three children of a sick widow.

The night before he died of polio on July 4, 1925, at age twenty-four, he wrote a note with a nearly paralyzed hand to a friend in the St. Vincent de Paul Society, asking him to deliver medication to a poor sick man he had been visiting.

Even his death was most likely brought on by his selfless charity. Doctors speculated that he contracted polio from some of the sick that he served. As his health rapidly deteriorated he kept his suffering hidden as he focused his depleted energy not on himself, but on others—especially his grandmother, who was dying at the same time he was.

Even Pier Giorgio's parents had no idea of the tremendous

self-emptying service he had given to Turin's poorest of the poor. The thousands of poor people who lined the street for his funeral procession genuinely surprised them.

The Eucharist fueled Frassati's life. Not only did he receive Communion daily, he would often spend long nights in fervent Eucharistic adoration. He was inspired by St. Paul's letters, especially 1 Corinthians 13, and by the writings of St. Catherine of Siena.

He prayed the rosary daily on his knees at his bedside. His father would often find him asleep in that position.

"He gave his whole self, both in prayer and in action, in service to Christ," wrote his sister, Luciana.

In his homily at the beatification Mass for Pier Giorgio, Pope John Paul II said: "Certainly, at a superficial glance, Frassati's lifestyle, that of a modern young man who was full of life, does not present anything out of the ordinary. This, however, is the originality of his virtue, which invites us to reflect upon it and impels us to imitate it…. His love for beauty and art, his passion for sports and mountains, his attention to society's problems did not inhibit his constant relationship with the Absolute. Entirely immerse in the mystery of God and totally dedicated to the constant service of his neighbor: with this we can sum up his earthly life!"

Questions for Individual Reflection or Group Discussion

Pope John Paul II said of Pier Giorgio Frassati: "By his example he proclaims that a life lived in Christ's spirit, the spirit of the Beatitudes, is 'blessed,' and that only the person who becomes a 'man or woman of the Beatitudes' can succeed in communicating love and peace to others." Reflect on your own living as a man or woman of the Beatitudes (Matthew 5:3-12) in both sports and life.

Are you poor in spirit—not clinging to earthly riches or glory but seeking what is truly valuable for you and for others?

Do you mourn—are you involved in the lives of others to the point that if all or part of a relationship is lost you feel a void?

Are you meek—in the original sense of the word? Today it often means weak and cowardly. In ancient times meekness described a quality of a strong horse. It was not wild and undisciplined, but learned to respond to its master's sway in the saddle, the touch of his knee—the master and horse worked as one when the horse learned to be "meek." Are you able to respond to the "master's touch" and work with God as one?

Do you hunger and thirst to do God's will, or are you hungry and thirsty for other things?

Are you merciful, able to forgive wrongs?

Are you pure of heart, desiring only what God desires for yourself and for others?

Are you a peacemaker?

Are you ever persecuted for doing God's will? If so, how do you respond in the face of persecution? What do you need to persevere in those times?

> "Blessed are you when they insult you and persecute you and say every sort of evil thing against you on account of me; rejoice and be glad, because your reward will be great in heaven." (Matthew 5:11-12)

BIBLIOGRAPHY OF WORKS CITED

Scripture texts from the Old Testament are from *The New American Bible,* copyright 1970 by the Confraternity of Christian Doctrine. New Testament texts are from *The New Testament: St. Paul Catholic Edition,* copyright 2000 by the Society of St. Paul.

Biographical information on Pier Giorgio Frassati is from FrassatiUSA.org

Augustine. *Confessions.* (Oxford: Oxford University Press, 1991).

The Catechism of the Catholic Church. (Washington, DC: United States Catholic Conference, 1994).

General Instruction of the Roman Missal, 2002.

Giamatti, A. Bartlett. *Take Time For Paradise.* (New York: Summit Books, 1989).

Hahn, Scott. *The Lamb's Supper: The Mass as Heaven on Earth.* (New York: Doubleday, 1999).

Merton, Thomas. *The Seven Storey Mountain.* (New York: Harcourt Brace Jovanovich, 1978).

Pope John Paul II. Address to the International Olympic Committee, May 27, 1982.

_____. *Ecclesia de eucharistia,* 2003.

_____. Homily from the Beatification Mass of Blessed Pier Giorgio Frassati, May 20, 1990.

_____. Weekly audience, February 20, 1980.

Pope Pius XII. *Sport at the Service of the Spirit,* July 29, 1945.

Sancta Missa, Rituale Romanum: Rite of Baptism of Children, 1962.

Will, George F. *Bunts.* (New York: Free Press, 1999).

ST PAULS